Praise for *First, Eat Y[...]*

First, Eat Your Frog centers on work/life integration processes in a more thought-provoking, studious manner than the usual discussions of work and parenting, and will appeal to mothers who are not just going to work, but cultivating a professional career and approach to work and life.

Libraries and readers who choose *First, Eat Your Frog* will find its drive towards enlightenment and pattern adjustment makes for a series of concrete reflections not just on the balancing act, but the process of creating more satisfying, fulfilling dual careers in motherhood and business achievement.

– DIANE DONOVAN, *Midwest Book Review*

The practical guide that everyone needs to make their lives feel manageable. Elizabeth Arleo writes from her perspective as a working mom, but her advice is so specific and realistic that it applies to women, men, parents, and single people alike. This is a must-read book for anyone who is trying to tame the chaos that is day to day life.

– EMILY TISCH SUSSMAN, family policy advocate, political strategist, founder and host of "She Pivots," the podcast in partnership with *Marie Claire* about women, their stories, and how their pivot became their success

The actionable guide that working mothers need to thrive. Weaving together expert tips and relatable perspectives, Elizabeth Arleo offers valuable insights to help navigate the tension between work and motherhood.

— Reshma Saujani, Founder, Marshall Plan for Moms and Girls Who Code, and bestselling author of *Brave Not Perfect*

Where other advice books tell you to 'be more intentional, "have a growth mindset," and plan your self-care, Arleo opens her calendar, brain, and heart to show you exactly how, synthetizing all the strategies she's tried, adapted, and mastered. She's created the secret sauce of "doing it all," or at least the closest thing we've got.

— Lauren Smith Brody, author of *The Fifth Trimester* and co-founder of the Chamber of Mothers

It's hard to imagine someone writing with greater authority than Dr. Arleo about how to balance the competing demands of career and motherhood with grace, sanity, and—yes—humor. *First, Eat Your Frog* is as generous as it is wise.

— David Millstone, Co-Chief Executive Officer, Standard Industries

This strong, slim volume is a treasure chest of sage advice, backed by research and experience, and delivered in a way that is immediately actionable. Read it with a pencil in your hand or a notebook at your side. You will find relatable discussions and simple, actionable advice born of thought, research, and experience. It is as if Elizabeth (Dr. Arleo) is at your side not only as a mentor and guide, but also as a friend and collaborator.

– SAMANTHA RAZOOK, Founder and CEO,
Curious Jane Magazine

Exactly what all of us overwhelmed, burned out moms desperately need. Elizabeth Arleo has crafted a step-by-step guide for balancing work and family life, all while finding some much-needed time for ourselves. This funny, practical, and sage guidebook is a must read for parents at all stages of the child-rearing/career conquering game.

– ERICKA SÓUTER, Author of "How to Have a Kid
& a Life: A Survival Guide"

Dr. Elizabeth Arleo's personal mentorship has profoundly influenced others. She helped guide my own academic journey, and her tactical approach to addressing the challenges of work life integration is highly effective.

– DR. GERALDINE McGINTY, Professor of Clinical
Radiology and Population Health Sciences, Weill Cornell
Medicine, and first female Chair of the American College of
Radiology's Board of Chancellors

FIRST,
EAT
YOUR
FROG

Library of Congress Control Number: 2022951075

ISBN (paperback): 978-1-956450-58-3
(eBook): 978-1-956450-59-0

Armin Lear Press Inc
215 W Riverside Drive, #4362
Estes Park, CO 80517

FIRST,
EAT
YOUR
FROG

And Other Pearls for
Professional Working Mothers

ELIZABETH KAGAN ARLEO, MD

For my girls,
Sophia, Michaela & Giordana

Contents

Introduction

Overwhelmed.

In my mind's eye, I can see myself at the kitchen table late at night, eyes bleary behind my glasses (although I usually wear contacts), tethered to my breast pump and hunched over my board review books. I can hear the repetitive noise of the pump itself, as I struggle to get enough milk for the baby tomorrow and study for my board exams coming up. I can taste the sips of cold water I took to hydrate and help stay awake. More than anything, however, I can feel the feeling of feeling overwhelmed by the personal and the professional. Have you ever felt that way as a professional working mother?

If yes, then you are not alone. According to a 2011 *Forbes Woman* study, 95 percent of working mothers felt overwhelmed by work, home, and parenting responsibilities[1]…and this was *pre*-pandemic. Pandemic era news headlines now routinely read " "Working moms are not okay." "Pandemic Triples Anxiety And Depression Symptoms In New Mothers." "Working Moms Are Reaching The Breaking Point." You can also see the problem in numbers: Almost 1 million mothers have left the workforce—with Black mothers, Hispanic mothers and single mothers among the hardest hit."[2]

My mission with this book, from one working mother to the next, is to help with the overwhelm.

As a radiologist specializing in women's imaging, I work mostly with other working women, many of whom already have children or look forward to doing so. In my capacity speaking with patients about their imaging results, particularly mammography and breast MRI, much of what I do is also help manage anxiety. I bring my experiences in both capacities to this book.

If you are looking to stop feeling overwhelmed with work and life; trying to solve the problem of frequently feeling behind or about to drop the ball at work or at home; wanting to change from often feeling behind and reactive to in control and on top of things; aspiring to have an intentional fulfilling calm personal and professional life; desperate for mental clarity, calm and confidence at work and at home; searching for simple pearls of wisdom to follow to achieve the aforementioned—and going through career and family building, as part of the "sandwich generation" taking care of young children and elderly parents–know that I tried many things before learning the lessons shared in this book.

Maybe you have tried skimping on sleep to get more things done, and yet that has not worked because that just makes you less productive. Maybe you have not been able to get what you want personally and professionally because of unrealistic standards at home and at work. Maybe you feel as though you don't have time for everything or anything. Maybe you struggle with building a career and a family at the same time. Maybe you are afraid of failing at work or at home or in both arenas. Maybe you wonder if you should stop working and devote that time to your kids, and yet you fear that you would miss the vocation in your life Although we may train for years at our professions, we receive little to no training on how to be a parent, let alone parent *and* work at the same time. Being a parent is the hardest job I have ever had and combining it with an already stressful professional job can result in feeling overwhelmed frequently. By the end of this book, I hope you will feel transformed from overwhelmed to calm(er), with a steady path forward at home and work.

This book is about work life balance, about striving for success in both arenas. You *can* succeed in both, and as a doctor and a mother I'm here to share pearls of wisdom on how do so. Ambitious, career-oriented women with families really can have it all when they follow the advice of trusted experts: both modern and ancient.

How this book was born

In 2019, I was humbled and honored to serve as the President of the American Association for Women in Radiology (AAWR), a professional organization founded in 1981 as a unique resource for "professional socialization" for women in the male-dominated field of radiology; the latter is still true today, as only approximately 25 percent of practicing radiologists are female. My presidential priority was to focus on improving parental leave in radiology, which I discussed in the context of an AAWR speed mentoring talk on developing short- and long-term goals at the 2019 annual meeting of the Radiological Society of North America (RSNA). In this speed mentoring set up, inspired by speed dating, each mentor sat for ten minutes at each table before getting up and rotating to the next. At the end of the hour, while again hydrating with a much needed glass of water after talking so much, I was approached by one of the organizers, a radiology trainee, who asked if I would be willing to give an expanded version of what I had just said in 2020 as part of AAWR's work-life balance series interviewing successful women in radiology; I agreed and we planned on the fall.

By the time October 2020 rolled around, the world had changed irrevocably due to the COVID-19 pandemic and yet what I said at the AAWR work-life balance event (held virtually with 250 registrants) was remarkably consistent; the same lessons stood. The following month, November 2020, I modified my talk to speak as part of Cornell's Dining with Doctors Series for underrepresented minority students in the greater New York City area considering applying to medical school; the same general lessons stood. Then the following month, in December 2020, my eldest daughter Sophia, age 12 at the time, gave me pause for thought: "you should write a book about being a working mother," she said one evening while we were reading together in bed, "You know, how you do it, as a mother *and* a doctor, how you do both, what you've learned since you had me." It was one of the most important things anyone has ever said to me, because as a working mother, I think many of us are frequently plagued with the worry, "am I a good enough mother?" or worse, "what can I do to be a more perfect mother?" While not presenting me with a perfect mother award, Sophia's comment seemed to suggest that I was achieving at least a passing grade. And I *had* learned a fair number of lessons in the 11-12 years since I sat late at night at that kitchen table, tethered to my beloved breast pump, lessons which I was noticing stood to the test of time and which I was apt to quote to my three daughters, hoping to prep them—albeit *way* in advance—with principles to help their future personal and professional lives be as successful and satisfying as possible. I also may be talking to myself out loud about what works to help keep overwhelm at bay in often intersecting personal and professional domains.

Furthermore, Sophia's comment caught my attention because it has been a huge life goal of mine to write and publish a book, in part inspired by my father, Joseph Arleo, who published two works of fiction, *The Grand Street Collector* and *Home Late*, in the early 1970s before going back to school to get his PhD in psychology in his forties, where he met my mother, Lillian Kagan, who was pursuing the same degree. In 2015, I participated in National Novel Writing Month (NaNoWriMo), the goal of which is to write a 50,000-word novel in one month. I chose to write a nonfiction family history instead for my girls, only Sophia and Michaela at the time (our third daughter, Giordana, was born in 2017). I not only cleared 50,000 words, but also the experience of NaNoWriMo taught me that I can write 1667 words per hour (50,000 words / 30 days = 1,667). So, I thought, "I know I can do that and publishing a book has been a huge life goal." At the time, I had more time at home due to COVID-19 than I possibly would when life goes back to normal, whatever the new normal may be. Finally, to quote the old Jewish proverb, if not now, when?

My answer to myself: now.

What becomes possible once these articulated lessons are considered together? OR the benefits of this book

Upfront, I want to be clear that I in no way want to insist that I have found the one, true way. Rather, I am a professional woman with a long-standing interest in organization, time management, and efficiency, which has only increased as I have had each of my three children, grown my career and continue to struggle with strong perfectionist tendencies. Along the way, I have learned—and am still learning—valuable lessons that have significantly helped me in the complexities of life as a professional working mother. I want to share them with others in my cohort in the hope that my insights might in some ways, big or small, ease the challenges faced by my fellow professional working mothers and help.

In other words, the benefits these eight "pearls" offer me, and which I hope they will offer you the reader, include: improved work-life balance or integration; a game plan for getting things done with greater ease and success, at work and at home; and greater self-confidence and self-care of yourself as a professional working mother.

In sum, in this book, I use what I have learned as a successful woman in radiology with three young children to help other similarly situated professional women achieve improved work-life integration and success.

How the book is organized

Chapters one through eight cover eight key lessons I have learned in my ongoing journey as a professional working mother, including:

1. Eat your frog

2. 168 hours - you actually have more time than you think

3. If you fail to plan, you are planning to fail

4. Remember the pre-meeting meeting…and that you are not an impostor

5. Don't let the perfect be the enemy of the good

6. Stop over-apologizing

7. It doesn't hurt to ask politely

8. Have a growth mindset

The Conclusion addresses ways to take these eight lessons from the book and into the world for practical use.

To quote Ecclesiastes 1:9, "There is nothing is new under the sun." In other words, many of the lessons articulated above and discussed in this book are attributed to wise women and men who have come before me and whose ideas have influenced my life. For example, the "Eat your frog" idea, hanging on my office wall, is attributed to Mark Twain, who supposedly wrote, "If it's your job to eat a frog, it's best to do it first thing in the morning. And if it's your job to eat two frogs, it's best to eat the biggest one first." Thus, chapter one discusses this idea, that if something is important, then try to do it at the beginning of the day, week, month, quarter, or year. Related to this, the pearl of chapter two—to think about time in terms of 168 hour chunks instead of 24—comes directly from the book "168 Hours" by author Laura Vanderkam; the pearl is that even if you work 50 hours and sleep 56 hours, then you still have 62 hours after work and sleep, so it is not accurate to say you do not have time for something. Rather, "I don't have time" means it is not a priority. Next, chapter three—if you fail to plan, then you are planning to fail (Benjamin Franklin)—covers practical planning strategies so you can choose your priorities and get them done.

Chapter four—remember the pre-meeting meeting and that you are *not* an impostor—conveys a vital lesson I first learned from one of my brilliant external mentors, Dr. Cheri Canon, Chair of the Department of Radiology at the University of Alabama at Birmingham, who made explicit the fact that men have pre-meetings in which they may discuss how they will vote with key talking points and women should do the same to prepare for important meetings; Impostor Syndrome, which even former first lady Michelle Obama speaks and writes about, can make any professional meetings more challenging. That being said, chapter five discusses Voltaire's important advice: don't let the perfect be the enemy of the good. Or as Sheryl Sandberg put it more recently, done is better than perfect. Related to this is the key idea of chapter six: stop over-apologizing; genuine apologies when appropriate are obviously crucial to interpersonal relationships, and yet over-apologizing, among other things, can be an unnecessary source of weakness, a habit to consider breaking.

I'm no Emily Post with respect to manners, and yet along the lines of how deportment can be helpful, chapter seven discusses how professionally and personally, it doesn't hurt to ask politely. Chapter eight covers the importance of a growth mindset, because as concept creator Carol Dweck wrote, with a growth mindset, "people believe that their most basic abilities can be developed through dedication and hard work—brains and talent are just the starting point. This view creates a love of learning and a resilience that is essential for great accomplishment."[3] The Conclusion will help you take the eight lessons learned into the world with you.

There are limitations to these pearls of wisdom. First, I acknowledge their sources are overwhelmingly white. This honestly came as a shock to me when, upon retrospective review, this came to my attention, because diversity, equity and inclusion are a central part of what I work on in radiology; specifically, I speak with and mentor underrepresented minorities in radiology; intentionally cultivate and have one of the most diverse editorial boards of radiology journals; and have led the American Association for Women in Radiology (AAWR), as women still remains a minority (again, only approximately 25%) of practicing radiologists. All I can say is that I know what I know; I do not want to pretend to know what I do not know or that what has been helpful to me comes from any sources other than what has organically occurred; yet this is a powerful reminder to me to include more diverse sources—authors like Tiffany Dufu with her impactful 2017 book, *Drop the Ball: Achieve More by Doing Less*—in my reading and writing. Second, it surprised me that several of the pearls originated from not only white men, but also old white men at that. Personally, as a working woman, why would I care what these men from a different time period, a different world, have to say, especially today when I generally look for more wisdom from women in my life? Well, that being said, there are reasons why Mark Twain, Benjamin Franklin and Voltaire are famous. Their words of wisdom have stood the test of time and endure perhaps *because* their advice is timeless. Furthermore, the efficacy of male mentors for female mentees has been documented in the literature and I have experienced this firsthand, in that, in my career I have been fortunate to benefit from the mentorship, sponsorship and wisdom of several male advisors senior to me. Yet it has been important for me to think about this and to reflect on why this is the case.

How I recommend reading the book

There are two ways of reading this book. One, read it straight through, start to finish, because the lessons are provided in a logical order. Two, after reading this introduction, jump to whichever chapter's lesson intrigues you the most; each chapter can be read on its own because each lesson makes sense and stands independently.

What I hope for you as you dive in

From one professional working mother to the next, my hope as you dive into this book is that you will find something that resonates with you, that is (relatively) easily actionable, and that will help you live a more satisfying and content personal and professional life. My promise to you is that the eight pearls curated and conveyed here will help you on your journey from overwhelm to greater calmness and clarity, personally and professionally.

1

Eat your frog

> *"If it's your job to eat a frog, it's best to do it first thing in the morning. And if it's your job to eat two frogs, it's best to eat the biggest one first."*
> —Mark Twain

One of the highest compliments I have ever received is that I'm a "frog-eater par excellence." Geraldine McGinty, MD, MBA, the first female chair of the American College of Radiology (ACR) Board of Chancellors, once wrote that about me. Geraldine is my breast imaging colleague at work, a mentor and sponsor, and a role model and professional friend. In the October 10, 2020 edition of her newsletter, in which she promoted my virtual American Association for Women in Radiology (AAWR) webinar on "Getting Things Done," she asked for a quotation as a teaser and I provided the one above by Mark Twain. Her endorsement included the compliment about my frog-eating abilities.

Little did she know that I almost *was* a frog eater—literally. More on that below. But first, an overview of this chapter's frog fundamentals.

Overview of chapter lesson

The purpose of this chapter is to chew over, so to speak, the eat-your-frog principle and how it operates. First, an anecdote of how I literally almost ate a frog in my striving for perfection as a mother (more on how *not* to do this in chapter five, don't let the perfect be the enemy of the good). Second, I'll dissect (again, so to speak) why eating your frog is important, or what happens when you don't apply this principle. Third, I discuss what I had to overcome to take the first step towards frog eating and what steps readers may take themselves.

How I almost ate a frog

Once upon a time, towards the beginning of the second quarter of 2020, our family went to Connecticut, decamping to a rural weekend home during the first peak of the COVID-19 pandemic. We set up shop to work remotely, brought my elderly parents with multiple comorbidities with us and felt incredibly grateful to be able to do so. Many cities, including New York City, were under shelter-in-place orders, and work to the extent possible and school became virtual. Nursery school for my youngest daughter, Giordana, age three at the time, was no exception, and the teachers valiantly continued teaching the spring curriculum remotely, focusing on the alphabet. "Homework" assignments each day focused on finding a tangible item that started with the letter of the day that would be studied the next. After A was for apple and B was for ball, C was for cookie and D was for dog (our black Labrador Lupa was virtually "showed and telled"), my perfectionist tendencies in the form of the desire for my three-year-old daughter to have "the best" example of a letter kicked in. Thus, on the way back from a morning run, I stopped by the nearby pond to catch the fattest F is for frog our family had seen. I put it into one of the many one-liter glass mason jars we have around the house and use for a variety of reasons—me mostly to try to meet daily water drinking goals.

A few hours later, we sat around the kitchen table for lunch, still a new experience for the family on a weekday. The sun streaked across the table in a warm glow, and I could have used my sunglasses. Ignoring the glare in my eyes, I sat down with a sandwich across from my three-year-old. "How was school this morning?" I asked, automatically reaching for the mason jar in front of me towards achieving my daily water intake goals and taking a sip. "Did you get up to F?"

Before I could hear Giordana's answer I almost spit across the entire table. I had just taken a large gulp from the mason jar containing the F is for frog. With the sunlight glinting off the glass and the plump amphibian probably desperately frog kicking the other direction away from my predatory gaping mouth, I had almost literally eaten my frog. I am not sure who was more traumatized, me or the animal in the jar that we soon after released back into its natural habitat.

Why frog eating (figuratively) is important— and what happens when you don't apply this principle

According to a 2009 article in *The Guardian* about frogs' (legs), "Belgium and Luxembourg are also noted connoisseurs, but perhaps surprisingly, the country that runs France closest in the frog import stakes is the US. Frogs' legs are particularly popular in the former French colony of Louisiana, where the city of Rayne likes to call itself Frog Capital of the World but are also consumed with relish in Arkansas and Texas, where they are mostly served breaded and deep-fried."[4] So, unless you are in one frog capital of the world on another, it is not that I literally recommend eating your frog as I almost did. Rather, in my opinion, this saying is important because it reminds us that we are human; that humans have strengths and weakness, the latter of which includes some degree of inertia, procrastination, or lack of will power. By figuratively eating our proverbial frogs, whatever they may be, we can acknowledge and choose to deal with these intrinsic weaknesses by getting the most important thing done up front.

To make a text-to-text connection between frogs and willpower, let's consider the children's book series, *Frog and Toad* by Arnold Lobel. In a chapter entitled "Cookies," the eponymous characters are enjoying homemade cookies by Toad, and at the same time having trouble limiting their intake – I can relate, can you? So, Toad says to Frog, "Let us eat one last cookie, and then we will stop." They eat one last cookie and yet there are many cookies left in the box, so Toad says to Frog, "let us eat one very last cookie, and then we will stop." Frog and Toad ate one very last cookie. "We must stop eating!" cried Toad as he ate another. "Yes," said Frog… "we need willpower,"[5] going on to define it for his amphibian friend and to take supportive steps—tying string around the box, then putting the box on a high cupboard shelf, and ultimately giving the cookies to the birds— to help them achieve it.

As defined by Arnold Lobel's Frog, willpower is trying hard *not* to do something you really want to do, and, to extend his definition, trying hard to do something you really want to do as well. In other words, by eating your frog—doing the most important thing first thing in or at the beginning of the day, week, month, quarter, or year—you make it as easy as possible to do something you really want to do or deem important for you to do personally or professionally. As a professional working mother, my interpretation of why eat your frog is so important is as follows.

First, by eating your frog first thing in the morning (or week or month), you set yourself up for success. How? In Chapter 3, "If you fail to plan, you are planning to fail," I share my methods for planning on a daily, weekly, monthly, quarterly basis and beyond. For now, though, however you plan what you want to get done personally and or professionally, if you choose to complete the most important thing as early as possible, then to echo *Annie* (the Broadway musical or subsequent 1982 and 2011 films), *come what may*, your day, week, month, quarter, or year has already been a success, no matter what else goes down.

If the most important thing is an inner expectation you've set for yourself, such as exercise, and you have no problem meeting outer expectations but struggle to meet your own interior ones, then set up a system of exterior accountability to help you get the job done, such as running with a friend or a joining a runners' group. I know the former is one of the few ways I've ever consistently run in the morning (I'm more naturally a night owl, despite many early mornings on various medical school rotations). More on this in Chapter 3.

Second, eating your frog lessens your mental load. According to ABC Health & Wellbeing, "The mental load is all the mental work, the organising, list-making, and planning, that you do to manage your life, and that of those dependent on you. Most of us carry some form of mental load, about our work, household responsibilities, financial obligations, and personal life."[6] The major component of my mental load in the personal arena since I became a mother is parenting, and maybe that is the same for you too. Components of your mental load in the work arena vary greatly depending on your profession. In academic radiology and academic medicine in general, the four components or "areas of focus" (a term from *Getting Things Done* by David Allen, more on that in the next chapter) include clinical work, administrative duties, research, and education—all of which have their associated mental loads. To remind myself to think through each area of focus professionally, I use the mnemonic CARE: Clinical, Administrative, Research and Education. Can you think of a mnemonic to summarize your work areas of focus? Is something in one of those areas weighing on your mind? Would you feel mentally unburdened if it was done and checked off your list? If yes, then that is your frog. In other words, eating your frog reduces your mental load because the most important or difficult task has already been accomplished and you no longer worry about it. Work from the National Counseling Society supports the idea of frog eating setting one up for success and lessening one's mental load, stating, "The more you procrastinate and leave the task undone, the more overwhelmed and stressed you are likely to feel about it...it's best to do it first thing in the morning to help gain a sense of momentum and accomplishment which, in turn, can help to reduce stress feelings."[7]

Professional working mothers often bear the lions share' of the mental load of parenting, which permeates throughout a workday when they are also handling professional areas of focus and the associated mental loads that entails. So not only after work may they come home to "the second shift," but also, they have a second mental load to carry *throughout* the day. "The second shift" is a phrase created by sociologist Arlie Hochschild which "refers to the household and childcare duties that follow the day's work for pay outside the home. While both men and women experience the second shift, women tend to shoulder most of this responsibility."[8]

However during the course of the COVID-19 pandemic where work and school became remote from home, these household and childcare duties for many women not only followed the day's work for pay outside the home, now rendered from the home due to shelter-in-place orders, self-quarantine, and new social distancing measures in the workplace and beyond; these duties became intertwined, and so were the associated mental loads, which thus increased.

Example of mental (over) load personally and professionally from my own life, August 2020, in the initial months after the COVID-19 crisis hit the United States: I was preparing dinner while listening to a conference call while my three-year old napped, muting and unmuting to drown out the sounds of questions from my older two ("What's for dinner? What time is dinner? Where is the soccer ball?"), but not thinking to do so when I had the water running while I washed my hands of the raw chicken I was preparing. The conference call leader said, "Where is that weird static coming from?" In lieu of a primal scream to release feelings of overwhelm / mental overload, I finished washing my hands of raw chicken and texted my AAWR colleague and friend on the call Lucy Spalluto MD, MPH, Associate Professor of Radiology at Vanderbilt University and Vice Chair of Health Equity, Director of Women in Radiology and Associate Director, Office of Diversity and Inclusion for the Department of Radiology, "The loud running water was me repeatedly washing my hands as I tried to get a chicken prepped and roasting in the oven while on our conference call while the baby naps," I wrote. To which Lucy replied, "I have a lovely visual of you wrestling the chicken on the phone, folding laundry, changing the world."

The above anecdote illustrates the very real multifaceted mental load that professional working mothers, and some fathers, bear—which in many cases was only exacerbated by the COVID-19 pandemic and the associated working and schooling from home. Roasting a chicken was not my frog (I like to cook) and neither was the conference call; I like and volunteer for the commission whose meeting I was attending. Rather, the confluence of the two demonstrates the often-overlapping items that need to get done at the same time and thus the sometimes double mental load that professional working mothers carry. Thus, one of my suggestions for lessening the mental load is eating your frog, so that whatever it may be, the most important thing personally and or professionally is not hanging over your head all day, week, month, quarter, or year, draining valuable mental energy that you could otherwise have. In other words, by eating your frog, you are lessening the mental load of your day and helping yourself to start off with a positive mental attitude, because you will have already achieved the priority of your day before the kids get up or you get to work or by noon. Depending on what your frog is, then, if possible, schedule it as early as possible. For example, dread going to the dentist? Schedule the appointment for yourself for Monday at 8 a.m. so instead of worrying about it all week, you've eaten your frog and will feel lighter not only for getting an important self-care task done, but also for having saved mental energy not anxiously anticipating it. For a larger project, for example, writing this book, I have scheduled it in the first quarter of the year, with the heaviest writing in the first month of the quarter, writing every single day, as early as possible.

In sum, what happens when you do not apply the principle of eating your frog is that not only are you *not* setting yourself up for success when you could be, but also you are losing valuable mental energy that you could otherwise retain. Scientific research is beginning to investigate this further, with a recent functional brain MRI study looking at "highlighting patterns of brain activations and autonomic activity when confronted with high mental workload" at the same time as other stressors."[9]

What you need to overcome to take the first step towards frog eating

What I had to overcome to take the first step towards frog eating is to overcome the natural procrastination that most of all of us have because we are human. According to Merriam Webster Dictionaries, to procrastinate is defined as "to put off intentionally the doing of something that should be done." Some people do this putting off only occasionally and others more frequently. Wherever you fall on the procrastination spectrum, self-knowledge about your tendencies – alluded to earlier in this chapter — can help you stop procrastinating and eat your frog, where the concept of the four tendencies comes from author Gretchen Rubin, who defines upholders as individuals who readily respond to outer *and* inner expectations; questioners as individuals who question all expectations and meet only those they believe are justified; obligers as individuals who readily meet outer expectations and yet have more difficulty meeting inner expectations; and rebels as individuals who resist meeting both outer *and* inner expectations. Based on these definitions, what is your tendency? According to Rubin's research, most people (41 percent) are Obligers, followed by 24 percent Questioners, 19 percent Upholders, and 17 percent Rebels.[10]

How does self-knowledge about your tendency help you to eat your frog? Well, if you are an Upholder, then deciding what your frog is and scheduling it as close to the beginning of a given time period will probably be enough for you to get your frog eating done, because Upholders usually meet inner (and outer) expectations and do not let themselves (or others) down. On the other hand, if you are a Questioner, then you might have to ask and answer for yourself *why* it might be important to eat your frog. The two reasons offered above (1) setting yourself up for success, and 2) lessening your mental load) might be sufficient, or you might need to generate additional justifying reasons yourself; when the *why* is internally sufficiently answered, then frog eating may follow. Contrastingly, Obligers need external accountability to get things done, so if you are an Obliger, then you might try making you inner expectation of frog eating (for example, exercise in the morning) an outer expectation (for example, run in the morning with friend or running group or trainer, who will be expecting you to show up). For Rebels to adopt frog eating, I would say consider the information provided as to why frog eating is important, as well as consequence of not-frog eating—failure and drain of energy that could otherwise be for freedom to choose what you want to do. It is your choice. If I am more dismissive in my explanation for this last category, it may be a combination of the fact that I myself (no surprise here) am an Upholder and that Rebels are not only the smallest group but also the tendency least likely to be interested in lessons learned (and thus this book), because they value self-determination.

Irrespective of tendencies, we are all human and thus all suffer from decision fatigue. In a 2020 article in *Medical News Today*, decision fatigue is defined as "a psychological phenomenon surrounding a person's ability or capacity to make decisions . . . [which] can get worse after making many decisions, as their brain will be more fatigued. This fatigue applies to all decisions, not simply the large or more difficult ones," going on to describe the decision-making ability as a finite source like a battery.[11] The reason I bring up decision fatigue is that its very existence provides another reason to decide what your frog is, and then eat it as close to the beginning of the day, week, month, quarter, or year as possible. In other words, to make bare the connection between decision fatigue and frog-eating, frog-eating accomplishes a priority before decision fatigue starts or sets in. Especially if your frog of the day—editing a book, having a difficult conversation, writing a report—involves numerous decisions, then the later you wait in the day to eat that frog, the more likely that the result will be poor, either due to impaired decision-making capabilities or due to doing nothing.

According to this *Medical News Today* article, there are several ways to combat decision fatigue. First one on the list? "Make important decisions first. If each decision depletes a person's energy, it may be best to make the most important decisions as early as possible each day. Whether it is a tough phone call, hard project, or another difficult task, making important decisions early in the day may help prevent decision fatigue when facing these choices." This is another way of saying eat your frog. Other suggested ways to combat decision fatigue include removing distractions, automating what you can (for example, wardrobe and meal planning) and taking breaks.

There are limitations to the eat-your-frog pearl of wisdom, primarily that, like most things in life, it is better in moderation. In other words, eat your frog should not be taken to the extreme whereby one only or always does challenging or difficult tasks, and never has time for the more enjoyable aspects of life. For a more balanced approach to life, I am certainly not advocating a puritanical approach of only hard work. Rather, to paraphrase a well-known proverb, "all work and no play makes Jane a dull girl," meaning without time off from work, a person becomes bored and boring. In sum, it is also important to let desire lead, as well as frogs.

Conclusion

The basic implication of the frog-eating lesson is this: figure out the most important thing you need to do in a given time period and then do it as close to the beginning of that time period as possible in order to set yourself up for success and lessen your mental load. The logical next step is to consider pearl numbr two, because after you eat your frog, you still have plenty of time to take care of your other most important personal and professional goals—and just knowing that you actually do have the time to do so can also help minimize the often-maximal stress professional working mothers experience.

2

168 hours—
you actually have more
time than you think

In June 2015, I discovered the principle spotlighted in this chapter's title while slowly jogging in New York City's blooming Central Park on the verge of another hot summer. I was listening to my first audible.com book while exercising, and it was Laura Vanderkam's 168 Hours: *You have more time than you think.*

First, let me give credit for the idea of listening to books while exercising to one of my college roommates, Kathryn, violist for a major metropolitan symphony orchestra and another professional working mother. Explained Kathryn, "Professionally, I play music all day, so when I go to exercise, I want a break, want to do something new. I love to read and listening to books 'on tape' while exercising is an engaging way to pair exercise with something I like to do while getting more reading done." In this way, Kathryn was also demonstrating that that you can *feel* like you have more time by pairing two things together: exercise and reading, but in

one instead of two time slots. This was valuable in and of itself and my knowledge and way of thinking about time was only further impacted by the first book I listened to.

Overview of chapter lesson

The purpose of this chapter is to convey the pearl of thinking about time in 168 hour chunks instead of 24. First, I'll summarize key ideas in Laura Vanderkam's 2010 book, *168 hours*. Second, I take a look at why I felt more time-starved before heeding the wisdom of "168 hours," followed by what I had to overcome to take the first step in following the principle. Finally, we focus on how you can use three questions to implement this lesson in your own life.

168 hours: key points

As the title and subtitle of Vanderkam's book suggest, we all have 168 hours per week and thus have more time than we think. How or why? Well, argues Vanderkam—a successful writer, speaker, podcaster, time-management expert and mother of five—even if, for example, you work as much as fifty hours a week and sleep eight hours a night seven days a week (sounds absolutely sublime to most professional working mothers), then you would still have [168-(50+56)=] 62 hours a week *after* working and sleeping for your family, for your friends, and for yourself. Thus, to say you do not have time for something just is not true; more accurately, it means that whatever you say you do not have time for is not a priority. That's fine. Identify the most important things that you want to do, because you do have time for them. Words matter.

Another important point Vanderkam makes is that we cannot be more efficient with our time if we do not know where our time is going. To figure out how we are spending our time, she advocates tracking your time for at least one week and tallying up general categories (for Excel or PDF time logs in 15- or 30-minute increments, see Vanderkam's website). She also advocates for thinking through an ideal realistic week—not a fantasy one sipping a favorite beverage on a desert island with a great book in hand (now you know mine), but rather one involving basic commitments (for example, sleep, kids, work) blocked out and additional things you would like to do regularly scheduled in as well.

Related to setting priorities, Vanderkam also advocates for making weekly and quarterly goals in the categories of Self, Relationships and Career. I find this framework helpful because it reminds me to consider these three major arenas in my life. On the topic of these three categories, Vanderkam comments that while the career category is self-explanatory, the categories of relationships and self are less straight-forward in terms of goal development, and yet, "Creating priorities in these categories forces a certain mindfulness in one's personal life. Putting a stake in the ground that something is important — that these categories deserve to have something important — increases the chances that such things happen. And that right there creates more work/ life balance."[12] Whereas Vanderkam tends to discuss these three categories above in alphabetical order (Career, Relationships, Self), since I'm an Upholder with some Obliger tendencies (such as people pleasing), as Rubin would say, in my weekly and quarterly planning I intentionally put Self first because it reminds me of the truth that if I want to optimally take care of others, both my personal relationships or my patients professionally, then I need to take care of myself first. If you also tend to put the needs of others before your own, then this might be helpful to you as well.

The cost of not heeding the wisdom of "168 hours"

Before I heeded the wisdom of "168 hours," I commonly felt like I did not have time to do all the things I needed to do, or I felt overwhelmed in the process of trying to do them. It is not that now I feel like I *always* have time to do the things I need or want to do, but rather, substantial pressure is lifted. In other words, thinking about time as 168 hours / week instead of 24 hours / day takes pressure off in terms of getting things done, because of the simple math that I have 60 plus hours after sleeping and working for myself and my relationships. More on this in Chapter 3, too.

When I didn't heed the call of "168 hours," the immediate cost was my sanity. In contrast, in heeding the call of "168 hours," when life feels out of control, like I can barely manage to get done everything I want to do, I open a new excel spreadsheet in Google docs and map out with color coding the most important things. More details on how to do this below; the important point here is that seeing 60+ hours of white space available *after* sleep and work is truly calming, because I see that in fact there is plenty of time to manage that which is important to me. There is time, and like money, I choose how to spend it. For example, in the professional realm, I chose to go to medical school to take care of patients – my work and working hours follow accordingly. In the personal realm, in contradistinction to growing up as an only child, I wanted and was able to have 3 myself—hence, my family time on typical "school night" evenings (featuring several sequential bedtime routines occupying most of the night) follows accordingly as well.

As I color block out a realistic week, I feel more in control of and satisfied with my life, personally and professionally. I truly feel more ready to "keep calm and carry on" with the most important things I choose to do. As has been written, and written well, "While money is a very useful resource, time is the most important thing a man can spend. It is finite and it cannot be gotten back. We must learn to use it wisely."[13]

What I had to overcome to take the first step of using time more wisely

What I had to overcome to take the first step in heeding the 168-hour principle: I had to 1) figure out my priority(s) by striving to be an essentialist, and 2) track or block out my time on a regular basis.

Essentialism

In his 2014 revolutionary book *Essentialism: The Disciplined Pursuit of Less*, author Greg McKeown's defines essentialism as "a disciplined, systematic approach for determining where our highest point of contribution lies, then making execution of those things almost effortless."[14] The core mindset of an essentialist, McKeown explains, is believing in individual choice, that we can choose how to spend out energy and time; recognizing we live in a noisy world and that very few things are actually important; and finally acknowledging trade-offs or opportunity costs.

To overcome the ways of the non-essentialist, McKeown recommends paying attention to your thinking and replacing "I have to" with "I choose to"; replacing "it's all important" with "only a few things really matter;" and substituting "how can I fit it all in" with "what are the tradeoffs?" or what is the most important thing I need or choose to do now or today? The non-essentialist, writes McKeown, often feels out of control, or feels overwhelmed and exhausted because she takes on too much. Sounds like an accurate description of many working mothers I know, including myself at times. Thus, now more than ever, I am striving to be an essentialist who chooses "carefully in order to do great work, feels in control, gets the right things done, experiences joy in the journey."[15]

On the other hand, after recommending *Essentialism* to my colleague and mentor Dr. Geraldine McGinty (of the frog-eater par excellence compliment), she made an excellent point about it in her March 20, 2021, weekly newsletter entitled, "Is saying no to work a luxury women can afford?" Writes Dr. McGinty, "As a follow up to last week's discussion of trying to focus, my colleague Dr. Elizabeth Arleo gifted me the audiobook of Greg McKeown's Essentialism. She knows me well, I listened to it at 1.5x! …The book urges a "less but better" approach to prioritizing one's time and that's all good. But. The examples he cites are almost exclusively white male leaders in the technology world and the author completely fails to address that the ability to say "no" at work is a luxury that most women and certainly those in less senior positions can rarely afford. I've been guilty of perceiving a "no" negatively so the book will be useful context for me to work through that and understand how that "no" can improve our team's performance."

That being said, to focus in on the importance of a "less but better approach to prioritizing one's time," the essential question of essentialism, so to speak is: What is the most important thing I need, or I choose to do now or today, this week, month, quarter, or year, for myself, my relationships, and my career?

Thus, combining the idea of "168 hours" and planning in the three categories of Self, Relationships and Career with the essential question of essentialism has been a winning combination for me. Each week, month, and quarter, I ask myself, what is the most important thing I need or chose to do today (or this week, month, or quarter) for myself, for my relationships and for my career? Then, I schedule it in—if it is on the calendar, then it is probably going to get done—as early in the week, month and quarter as possible in order to eat my frog and set myself up for success by getting done as early as possible the most important thing.

Once you determine your priority for your day, week, month, quarter, or year, for your core categories of self, relationships, and career, how to schedule each priority into the time we have? Here is where we circle back to time tracking, as recommended by Laura Vanderkam.

Time tracking or blocking

I strive to track or block my time monthly to quarterly. In time blocking, I think intentionally about my "dream routine" for a realistic week and all it entails, personally and personally, using an Excel spreadsheet and assigning each entry a different color for ease of visualizing. First, I block out eight hours of sleep (11 p.m. – 7 a.m.) seven days a week in a light gray, like a computer or device going to sleep. Why? Well, without sleep, nothing else is going to happen as well as it should. More for myself later, but first sleep.

As an aside, as a physician, I can tell you that my colleagues who are sleep experts note that regularity in your sleep schedule supports quality sleep. The idea of making up for a sleep deficit—thinking, for example, you can catch up when the kids are at the grandparents' house this weekend—is a flawed concept.

What to block out next? I agree with Vanderkam that most people have no problem figuring out what needs to (or should) get done at work. Thus second, I block out my core work professionally in order of importance. As a physician, the most important thing I do professionally is take care of patients, so I start professionally by blocking out "Clinical" in dark gray, darker than the "sleep shade," because like sleep, this time is grayed out – nothing else can be scheduled here; if I must confess my level of detail, I further specify the service I am covering such as — and this is radiology specific — "Clinical: Breast MRI" or "Clinical: Body Ultrasound," for example. If you are a physician in an academic environment like I am, then you will also want to block out time—in keeping with trying to be a "quadruple threat"—for administrative duties (including meetings such as "tumor boards"), research, and education. If you are not a physician, then what is the most important thing you do? Color block this out in dark gray, or whatever other color resonates with you for work, along with the subsequent top two to three other professional activities you do as well.

Third, I color block out Relationships. This is more colorful. Each of my children has their own signature color, which I use for everything from calendar items (for example, if I put in "Dentist" in green, then I know this is for Sophia) to travel bags. So, I block out 7-8 p.m., in purple, for Giordana, my youngest, for focused, one-on-one play, bath, books, bed. Next, I block out 8:00-8:30 pm in pink (for love :) for my husband, for catching up (in a less interrupted way than, say, family dinner) on the couch and reading the newspaper, while our older girls do homework. Then, in ascending age order, I block out 8:30-9:30 p.m., in blue, for Michaela, my middle daughter, for one-on-one time together, her choice; sometimes we play cards or a game (Bananagrams and Boggle are two favorites), sometimes we just read our own books next to each other. Next, I block out 9:30-10:30 p.m., in green, for Sophia; usually I'm either writing in my planner, reading fiction or struggling (depending on the day of the week) to do *The New York Times* crossword puzzle in her bed while she finishes her homework at her desk and gets ready to bed. By this point, after having put three people to bed, I am pretty zonked myself; nothing much productive is going to be done in the next half hour before my self-imposed bedtime of 11pm, so I leave 10:30-11 p.m. as white space as a buffer or time for reading; more on this below. This is all for weekdays or school-nights; weekends are relatively more flexible, with more time blocked out for family adventures and my husband. Specifically, I block out Saturday evening starting at 6 p.m. for our weekly date night; it doesn't happen every week, but more weekends than not it does because it's on the calendar. I also block out times for family meals, generally at 6/7 p.m. and then time to visit my parents each week as well.

Finally, I block out time for myself. As an academic physician striving to be a "quadruple threat" in clinical, administrative, research and educational arenas, as an individual I like the tripartite framework of mind-body-spirit or physical-emotional-intellectual; make it a quadruple as well if you add the spiritual. For example, my annual goals for myself from 2021 and part of 2022 in these three categories included:

- For mind or intellect 2021, my goal was to write this book. I blocked out 30 minutes on my "dream routine" for "write or edit," Monday through Friday.

- For body or physical, my 2021 goal was to continue my running (and with it, reading) streak. I blocked out 30 minutes on my "dream routine" for "read and run," Monday through Sunday, seven days a week, during which time I could get through non-fiction reading on audible.com while I jogged.

- For spirit or emotional, my 2022 goal was to decrease my phone usage. To make this a SMARTER goal—where SMARTER is a mnemonic for Specific Measurable Actionable Risky (don't make it to easy, make it a bit of a stretch) Time-Keyed Exciting Relevant—I specified for myself, "Decrease my phone usage daily to <2 hours and <58 pickups." (Rationale for the later: According to 2022 statistics regarding time spent on smartphone, people check their phones on average 58 times every day.[16] This is problematic because, according to a study out of the University of California at Irvine, if you have been distracted from a task – say by picking up your smartphone – then it takes over 23 minutes on average to get back to deep focus.[17] Not good for productivity. This was one instance in which I want to be *below* average.) My key motivations are that I feel less scattered and more present when I am not on my phone; when I am at work, I truly want to focus; when I am away from work, I truly want to disconnect; and finally, I want to lead by example for my daughters, the next generation of smart phone users. To help me achieve this goal, I try to keep my phone out of site and/or reach; I put an automatic reply "OOO" message on my work email from Friday at 5 p.m. to Monday at 8 a.m. saying I am away from work until Monday morning; if the matter is urgent and cannot wait until that time, them please call me (and I provide my cell number); and since this is a daily habit, and in fact one I am trying to spend less time on instead of more, no time blocking is needed on my color-coded "dream routine." On the other hand, if you would like to develop a prayer or meditation habit daily, then you could block out time to do so for yourself, specifically for your spiritual or emotional well-being.

In all of this, I intentionally try to keep some white space on the calendar for three reasons. First, white space on the calendar creates a buffer, the presence of which may decrease stress in and of itself. Second, white space on the calendar allows for "known unknowns." More on this in the next chapter, but for now suffice it to say that the latter are seemingly infinite in both medicine and in dealing with children. Third, white space on the calendar tells me that I have room to expand: I'm not crowded in by everything I need to do, that I have space in the form of time, that most elusive and precious commodity. Why is time so precious? As one anonymous source wrote, "The greatest gift you can give someone is your time. Because when you give your time, you are giving a portion of your life that you will never get back."[18]

What I learned from 168 hours, and how the reader can use three questions to implement this lesson in ones' own life

What I learned from Vanderkam's book is what is articulated in the subtitle: "You have more time than you think." You can avoid the opposite, thinking you have less time than you have, by asking yourself the following questions, which were also inspired by her work:

1. What is the most important thing I need or choose to do today or this week, month, quarter, or year in the categories of self, relationships, and career? Write the answers down, possibly in a one sentence journal or a planner if you are still using paper to some degree (more on planners in the next chapter).

2. What is an ideal and real weekly schedule? Consider color blocking out your "dream routine." There may

be many versions, which evolve month to month or quarter to quarter, or your version may be relatively constant for a season of your life.

3. What can I do to get as close as reasonably achievable to the answer to #2? In other words, try to reconcile your current reality with your normative schedule.

There are limitations to the "168 hours" pearl of wisdom. Sometimes, even with the most intentional and beautiful color-blocked schedules, life serves up curve balls such as serious illness or injury, personally or in an immediate family member, and the associated emotional stress; unexpected urgent and important work deadlines; or financial crises that cannot be resolved in 24 or 168 hours. What to do then? In brief, recognize and acknowledge that for some time – but some time that will likely eventually pass – you will not be living your ideal week. You may need to re-evaluate your weekly, monthly, quarterly and annual priorities, and that is not a bad thing. Life is dynamic and so are our real ideal weeks. Goals are not written in stone; they can be revised, as can your color blocked schedule if you find it helpful. First and foremost, however, remember to keep sufficient sleep on there; without this basic element of self-care, you cannot optimally take care of others or your own goals.

Conclusion
The purpose of this chapter was to explore this important idea of 168 hours. The principal finding is that thinking of time in 168

instead of 24-hour blocks takes pressure off in terms of getting things done, because of the simple math that even if I were to work 50 hours and sleep 56 hours a week, then I would still have 62 hours left per week for my relationships and myself. The practical lesson of this finding is that you do, in fact, have more time than you might think. How to plan to use it? Thus, a logical next step is to consider the topic of the following chapter, per Benjamin Franklin: "if you fail to plan, you are planning to fail."

3

If you fail to plan,
you are planning to fail

"If you fail to plan, you are planning to fail."
— Benjamin Franklin

I do not remember the moment I first heard this quotation, but whenever I did, it certainly resonated with me. Some people are more naturally planners, while others are more "go with the flow;" both have advantages and disadvantages, and in either case, like it or not, I am definitively in the first camp. Actually, though, I do like it. For Upholders, "discipline equals freedom," is in fact a very good motto, as suggested by former Navy SEAL Jocko Willink in his 2017 book by the same name.[19] Furthermore, in my opinion, for working mothers, the discipline of planning will enable more personal and professional freedom, as I will discuss in this chapter. In other words, I would posit that, whichever camp you are in, when it comes to being a professional working mother, it is worth considering doing a bit more planning because if you do so, then

you may have more time to in fact go with the flow down the river of life instead of reactively putting out fires; this is particularly true if or when you have young children.

At a greater level, Franklin's call to action in terms of planning is about intentionally living our lives. It is about striving for order and purpose, not that it is always achieved or always clear. Consider the converse of Franklin's statement in that most people do not plan to fail; rather, they fail to plan…and the result may be failure or lack of success, in whatever was hoped for. Failure may still happen with planning, and yet with planning there is a greater chance of success and or learning lessons from mistakes. Specifically, and circling back the previous chapter, planning is about thinking through in advance how to intentionally use the time we have for our top priorities.

By way of overview, first I will provide additional context and history regarding Franklin's quotation and related sayings. Second, I will summarize my planning resources. Third, I will discuss how I put these resources into practice with an in-depth review of how I do planning in the short, medium, and long term. Finally, I answer questions regarding tried-and-true planning methods.

Planning: More context and history

Strategic planning has its origins in the military. "Picture generals poring over maps, meeting with their troops to discuss the plan… then evaluating what went wrong or right," describes CEO Jacob Engle, noting that the same goes for business, and yet he often hears business owners pushing back on this, "saying, "Isn't it easier to just shoot from the hip or lip?" Can't we just make it up as we go along? Who has the time to do this not-so-exciting, tedious work.""[20]

I often hear from working mothers' variations of the above

by Engel. This is understandable, and yet, if you fail to plan effectively—where effectively is different for each person and situation—there may be painful but potentially avoidable consequences for you and others, including your children. For example, if you fail to plan for a project at work, then execution may take longer than estimated, you get home later than expected, your babysitter is angry, your partner is annoyed, your child is aggrieved and already asleep and thus unable to ask you if you picked up the cupcakes for the school event tomorrow, so the next morning you have to stop on the way to school, making her late for school and you late for work, and then your boss and colleagues are irate. Any slice of this sound familiar or possible? If yes, then that is also understandable because I think most working mothers have been there in one form or another. Yet, it is an unhappy cycle you can stop, or at least minimize, by planning.

That being said, planning is necessary but not sufficient to ensure success because, as translated from Scottish poet Robert Burns, "the best laid plans of mice and men (sic) often go awry." In other words, even the best made plans can still go wrong. Traffic. Sick caregiver. Computer issues. All of the above. The possible list is infinite. So, knowing both one and two—where one is defined as "if you fail to plan, you are planning to fail," and two is defined as "the best laid plans...often go awry"—what can you do? Enter number three, where number three is: Build a buffer, expect the unexpected, and prepare for known unknowns. Let's look at each one of these in turn.

Build a buffer

First—and no you are not back in a high school chemistry class— let us consider the idea of buffers. In *Essentialism: The Disciplined Pursuit of Less*, Greg McKeown devotes a whole chapter to the topic of buffers, writing, "The only thing we can expect (with any great certainty) is the unexpected...we can either wait for the moment and react to it or we can prepare. We can create a buffer...defined literally as something that prevents two things from coming into contact and harming each other."[21]

Acids and bases from high school chemistry again aside, what are practical ways can we create a buffer? Four practical ways include:

1. Include white space on your calendar
   (as discussed in Chapter 2);

2. On your to do list, include time estimates—
   and err on the generous side;

3. Don't forget about load times;

4. Do scenario planning.

White space was discussed at the end of Chapter 2. Regarding time estimates on a to do list, McKeown of *Essentialism* recommends adding 50 percent to your time estimates. Why? Because of the phenomenon known as "planning fallacy," a term coined by renowned psychologist Daniel Kahneman in 1979 to refer to "people's tendencies to underestimate how long a task will take, *even when they have actually done the task before.*"[22] The concept of load times comes from the book *Managing Life with Children* and it is simple but effective: If it takes twenty minutes to get to school (and you add a buffer by adding 50 percent to your time estimate and make it thirty minutes), and you need to *actually* leave at 8 a.m., then consider 7:55 am your load time if you need five minutes to get everyone onto the car or to the school bus for actual departure. In our home, during the school year, the school bus arrives for the youngest at around 8:05 a.m.; thus 8:00 a.m. is the "load time"—and since everyone, including me, is tired of hearing raised voices for shoes, backpacks, and coats, at 8:00 a.m. I ring a bell to minimize words and maximize action.

What exactly is scenario planning and why do it? To answer the latter first, whether you are a glass half full or half empty kind of gal, scenario planning allows you, to quote the eighteenth-century English proverb, to "hope for the best, plan for the worst." This means that you can still be optimistic and at the same time prepare for possible less-positive outcomes. Derived from methods of military intelligence, scenario planning is a method used to make flexible long-term plans. While typically for organizations, McKeown and others espouse it for individuals as well. "The goal is to envision possible futures, which will serve as guideposts to the path forward," explains Peter Schwartz, cofounder of the Global Business Network in a 2009 *Wired* magazine article, describing the process as starting with a question and then, "Once you've formulated the issue, the method is simple: Identify forces likely to bear on the problem, organize them into future possibilities, envision paths that would lead to those futures, and devise a strategy for surviving them all."[23] Can you think of an example in your life now where scenario planning might be helpful?

Of note, I do want to mention, given the origin of scenario planning in military operations, that not all — and arguably not most — scenario planning on the home front needs to have military-level precision. In fact, in most cases, as discussed further in Chapter 5, this is a good time to remember, "don't let the perfect be the enemy of the good." That being said, the origins of ideas are both interesting and important for context and related relevance.

Expect the unexpected

Remember the book you may have read when pregnant, *What to Expect when You're Expecting*? Well, in my opinion, a good title for a sequel could be *With Children, Expect the Unexpected*, an idea which is compounded if you are a working mother as well. The earliest reference to "expect the unexpected" I could find comes from a quotation from Oscar Wilde's play *An Ideal Husband*: "To expect the unexpected shows a thoroughly modern intellect."[24] I do agree with playwright Wilde here and urge, as part of planning, so as not to fail to show a "thoroughly modern intellect," to expect the unexpected as you plan. Closely related to the idea of expecting the unexpected is the idea of known unknowns.

Known unknowns

At a February 2002 news briefing, then Secretary of Defense Donald Rumsfeld explained the limitations of intelligence reports: "There are known knowns. There are things we know we know. We also know there are known unknowns. That is to say, we know there are some things we do not know. But there are also unknown unknowns, the ones we don't know we don't know."[25]

In sum, if you do not heed to call to plan, it can lead to potentially unnecessary failure, potentially in that not all failure can be prevented (and sometime failure can be helpful, although that is beyond the scope of the current discussion). Yet by planning with a buffer, including scenario planning, we as working mothers drastically reduce the chance of it, of failing ourselves and our close relationships.

What I had to overcome to take the first step: Planning resources

What I had to overcome to take the first step in planning was to find a simple, reliable planning method that works for me personally and professionally, which is flexible to accommodate all that life as a professional working mother may involve, now and in the future, including in times of an unremitting global pandemic. After a long-standing interest in organization, dating back to a study skills class in primary school and reading many intervening articles and books on the subject subsequently, I read *Getting Things Done* by David Allen in 2010 and found my core methodology. I have been using GTD continuously ever since, tweaking it along the way with contributions from other resources I have found helpful in maximizing my efficiency and sanity.

My objective now is that by the end of this chapter, you will have a list of go-to resources to improve your planning, both in the short and long term, and understand how you might implement some of these resources, should you choose to do so. I often like to look at issues through the traditional journalist's framework of the 5Ws and an H (who, what, when, where, why and how). So, to put planning in this framework, I would say that in terms of *who*, developing short- and long-term goals, or engaging in planning for the short and long term, is probably useful for just about everyone. Skipping what for the moment to go to *when*, to be effective, planning is most effective when it takes place routinely, ideally daily, weekly, monthly, quarterly, and annually. In terms of *where*, I would say actually where is less important that having a consistent place, be it your kitchen table with a strong cup of coffee first thing in the day or in a comfortable chair with a relaxing cup of tea at the end; or weekly at your home and or work inbox to process paperwork and lists; or monthly or quarterly somewhere off-site (which I define realistically not as a desert island, but just not my home or work office in order to have neutral or different surroundings for optimal creative thought and reflection). In terms of *why* develop goals or why plan, I would say that planning is important in general because time passes, so to maximize personal and professional satisfaction and achievement, you might as well use time intentionally. More specifically, as a physician, when I find it difficult to stop thinking about a patient whose care I've been involved in (via image interpretation and management recommendations, or consulted about), particularly patients with late stage and or unexpected disease, I think about what lessons can be gleaned, because I am acutely aware that but for the grace of some higher being (if you believe in one) I could have potentially been this patient, and one day I may be this patient – repeatedly, the lesson learned I come back to in these situations is to live life intentionally, so as to make the most of the mortal and limited time each one of us has on this earth.

In terms of *what* I use to plan, my top three resources include the GTD methodology, the low-tech paper Full Focus Planner, and the high(er) tech app ToDoIst, each one described below; in subsequent sections I will cover *how* I put the resources into practice.

Getting Things Done (GTD)[26]

In 2001, David Allen published his now famous book, *Getting Things Done: the Art of Stress Free Productivity*, detailing his work-life management system based on the idea that, "your mind is for having ideas, not for holding them." The fundamentals of GTD involve 5 steps to "apply order to chaos": capture, clarify, organize, reflect, and engage. Capture means writing, recording or gathering "any and everything that has your attention into a collection tool," such as a physical or electronic inbox and/or a to-do list. Clarify means deciding if each captured item is actionable (if yes, then decide the next action or project it should be assigned to) or not (if not, then delete, defer, or save for reference). Organize means putting actionable items where they belong, including on future dates in electronic or paper calendars. Reflect means routinely reviewing lists of next actions daily, projects weekly, spheres of responsibility monthly, and annual goals on a quarterly basis, as well as taking dedicated time to think about longer time horizons and ultimately one's purpose in or vision for life. Finally, engage means doing the next delineated action(s) with confidence, because you can trust in the aforementioned system of organization that you are doing what you should be doing when and where you should be doing it.

Described as both a personal productivity and time management system, two of the most important elements in the GTD method—and this may particularly appeal to professional working mothers, I know it certainly does to me—are control and perspective. In terms of control, this come from utilizing the same above described 5-step workflow no matter what you are tackling; whatever comes up at work or at home, you have a simple 5-step method for processing anything and everything. In terms of perspective, GTD promotes reflection (step 4) from six levels or "horizons of focus," where the ground level encompasses all your immediate upcoming calendar and daily to-do list items that take only one action (e.g., call my mother); horizon 1 is projects (anything that takes more than one action to complete; most people have 30-100; GTD recommends reviewing weekly); horizon 2 is spheres of responsibility (most people have 4-7; review monthly); horizon 3 are goals and objectives in the next 1-2 years (review quarterly); horizon 4 is your 3-5 year vision (review annually); and horizon 5 is your purpose in work and in life (profound reflection). With greater control, gained from the routine use of the 5 fundamental steps for processing anything and everything (capture, clarify, organize, reflect, and engage), there is more time and mental space to move to broader horizons, so to speak, in this bottom-up approach.

In sum, if you choose to plan, then planning to use the GTD method ensures a flexible reliable system. The methodology has worked for me for over a decade now, and I give it my highest recommendation.

Full Focus Planner (FFP) [27]

In 2017, Michael Hyatt first sold his now famous full focus planner (FFP), a quarterly paper agenda that leads users through a 3-part framework, starting with the delineation of 8-12 annual SMARTER goals (with 3 or less assigned to each quarter as the "Quarterly Big 3"); followed by each of the Quarterly Big 3 being broken down into weekly objectives ("Weekly Big 3"), and finally daily actions ("Daily Big 3"). In this system, your 3 main daily goals are derived from thinking about what next actions will help you achieve your 3 main weekly goals, which are derived from thinking about what next actions will help you achieve your 3 quarterly goals, which stem directly from your annual SMARTER goals. Along the way, the paper planner takes you through a weekly (p) review, with space to note how far you got on your Weekly Big 3, reflect on your biggest wins, what went well and what didn't, what you want to keep or improve, start or stop doing, as well as how you want to eat, sleep, move, connect and relax. Each planner is for 90 days, one quarter, with each day spread out over two pages, the right-hand side lined but otherwise blank for taking any pertinent notes in meetings or calls that happen that day and the left-hand side including a bulleted checklist (next to space to write in the Daily Big 3) to indicate completion of morning and evening rituals, and workday startup and shutdown rituals, with dedicated pages at the beginning of the planner for writing the elements of each ritual with time estimates; it is also just the size of a book, so can easily be taken along wherever you go, for easy utilization. Since it's a paper planner, it also helps decrease screen time.

Two of the most important elements in the full focus method—and this may also particularly appeal to professional working mothers, I know it certainly does to me—are incremental progress and reduction of burnout. With respect to the former, as professional working mothers, we probably do not have large chunks of white space on our calendars each day to get things done. And yet we may have scattered smaller pieces of time, 15, 30 or even 60 minutes where we can get things done if we are intentional about our time and focus. Enter the Full Focus Planner. Decide what the three most important things you need to get done that day are, commit to them by putting them in writing in your Daily Big 3, and then if/when you have 15, 30 or even 60 minutes free, focus on getting those things done. Circling back to entering time estimates with tasks, this is another place where doing so shows its value, because you can match time available with time to complete task.

With respect to reduction of burnout, this is important now more than ever as health threats such as COVID continue to impact the way we interact and function. For physicians specifically, the American Medical Association has reported that nearly 30 percent of all physicians experienced high stress related to COVID-19 and 29 percent had substantial levels of work overload.[28] For all women more generally, a 2022 study of 5,000 women across ten countries first reported by ABC news noted that 53 percent of working women reported stress levels higher than one year prior, with mental health declining and work-life balance becoming nearly "nonexistent."[29] Long to-do lists contribute to overwhelm and they, in turn, contribute to burnout. The

FFP helps you narrow your list, and thus your overwhelm and burnout, by providing a simple method to articulate, from the top down—where the top is the annual goals you set for yourself—what your Quarterly Big 3 goals are, which dictate your Weekly Big 3 goals, which dictate your Daily Big 3 goals. Following this prioritization system ties back to essentialism and goal setting in the three domains of Self, Relationships and Career as well.

ToDoIst

ToDoIst is a project management application for productivity, personal and professional, allowing users to manage their tasks from a smart device or computer at little to no cost. With the app, tasks in ToDoIst can be categorized by projects or sit loosely in an inbox as they come to mind, allowing you to get them out of your head, ala Allen's *Getting Things Done*. Projects can be location-based (e.g., @ home, @ office, @ errands) or medium-based (e.g., @ call, @ email, @ text) [See Figure 1]. Tasks can then be filtered by project or date. As I enter a task in my ToDoIst, I categorize them by project, give them a date (when I will do it), and put my time estimate in parentheses next to it, erring towards the side of a more generous time estimate than a cheap one (*a la* McKeown's *Essentialism* advice to add 50 percent to time estimates). In this way, I can look at my daily ToDoIst in conjunction with my Full Focus Planner's Daily Big 3, tally up how much time everything should take, compare it to how much time I have to get things done and if it is not somewhat similar, then I need to make some adjustments to set myself up for success.

Putting it into practice: *how* I actually do my planning

Having discussed my top three resources with respect to

planning, organization and getting things done—GTD, FFP, and ToDoIst—I will now turn to *how* I use these resources to specifically do my planning in the short and long term. While no method is full proof, I have found that using the bottom-up GTD methodology with the top-down FFP in conjunction with the digital ToDoIst together makes for a highly reliable system, even if I don't hit every component every time I ideally plan to do so.

Short term planning: daily and weekly

When: I block out 5:30-6:00 p.m. on my calendar for daily planning, the elements of which are articulated in my FFP daily rituals page and incorporate those of my workday shutdown ritual; this is my preferred time, because it helps me feel more comfortable closing down work for the day, knowing that I've done what I needed to do today and have specific plans for what I need to do tomorrow – in effect, it allows me to give permission to myself to be less achievement-orientated for the rest of the day and more just present with my family (although this mental switch of gears can be easier said than done when, as a professional working mother, you feel sometimes like your to-do list is Sisyphean). If, for whatever reason, it does not happen (expect the unexpected), then Plan B is to complete my daily planning at 9:30-10:00 p.m., while my eldest is completing her homework. I often make minor tweaks to the specifics to meet changing needs, however the basic plan is largely the same: with my FFP and smart phone in hand, I do my workday shutdown, which currently includes: CTEP – Calendar, ToDoIst, Email and (Full Focus) Planner. I try to get this daily planning done in thirty minutes, but being gentle with myself, that doesn't always happen (so if I start at 5:30 and have a hard stop at 6 p.m. but am not finished, then I can complete at 9:30 p.m.).

- **Calendar**: review the day just finished to see if there are any loose ends I need to tie up, and then review the next day and the day after, setting alarms on my phone as needed before important meetings and events. The idea to prep two days in advance comes from my training as a breast imager, where we prepare for patients undergoing localizing procedures at least two days in advance so that if any images or reports are missing, there is a buffer in between so all missing items can be obtained prior to the actual procedure. For example, for kids playdates on the calendar, 1-2 days beforehand, I send a confirmation email or text to the parent of the child about the playdate, then email the teacher about dismissal plans if needed, and then email or text whoever is doing the pickup to make sure no child is left behind. I do this first, pre-ToDoIst, so that if I send out questions, some answers hopefully come in while I'm looking at ToDoIst.

- **ToDoIst**: I review the day just finished to see if there are any items I still need to complete, and then review the next day and the day after, trying to ensure that my Daily Big 3 are clear and that all items have time estimates.

- **Email**: I strive for inbox zero by the end of the week when I do my weekly(p)review, and for the end of the day, I strive to color code any remaining emails in my inbox (ideally ten or less) so I know the disposition, such as red (do tomorrow), orange (research), yellow (do this week), green (do next week), blue (Clinical

Imaging, the radiology journal for which I'm Editor-in-Chief), purple (waiting for), pink (save for future reference). Not surprisingly, of CT/EP, E for Email takes up the most time.

- **Planner**: In the "other tasks" small lined section of the Full Focus Planner, I then reflect on my day with the mnemonic BLUG (like blog): Biggest wins (2), Lessons learned (2), Unfinished business (2), Grateful for (2) and write in my Daily Big 3 for the next day, drawing from my Weekly Big 3 (which draws from my Quarterly Big 3, which draws from my self-articulated Annual Goals) and ToDoIst.

Weekly planning for me takes place on Thursday or Friday afternoon, a time which tends not to be otherwise highly productive, and I block out 60-120 minutes for it. Weekly planning incorporates my CTEP (Calendar / ToDoIst / Email / Planner) daily approach, and adds in David Allen's Step 1 "collect" by emptying my work bag and any other bags used in the past week, as well as my physical inbox, which is my catch all for mail, bills and everything and anything that comes in during the week that I can't delete, do in two minutes, or delegate quickly. In sum, using the Full Focus Planner Weekly (P)review as a guide, I:

- **Clear** bags, desk clutter & physical inbox
- **Calendar**: review the next week to get a lay of the land
- **ToDoIst**: review the next week to get a lay of the land
- **Email**: get to inbox zero, professionally and in my Gmail

- **Planner:** follow the Full Focus Planner Weekly (p) review, called a (p)review because you both review the week you are wrapping up (including, biggest wins; how far you got on your Weekly Big 3 goals, what worked and what didn't, and daily notes pages to see if there are any action items) and preview the week upcoming by putting into writing what you want to KISS (where KISS stance for Keep Improve Start Stop) and setting your Weekly Big 3 goals, which I do in the three categories of Self, Relationships and Career (while still working towards my Quarterly Big 3 goals, which again come from my annual goals list).

- **Photos purge:** on phone, delete any bad ones taken in last week so when I do my monthly upload and backup to Snapfish (the online photo website I've been using for over two decades), I am just adding good photos that I actually want.

- **OOO:** finally, and this is a recent addition to help me maintain better boundaries and not work when I'm officially off, I turn on a "automatic reply" on my work email, starting Friday at 5 p.m. and stopping on Monday at 8 a.m., with the message stating: "I am away from work until Monday morning. If this is an urgent matter which cannot wait until that time, then please call me (cell number provided)." With this automatic reply, I am giving my permission to truly disconnect from work and try to recharge over the weekend, while knowing that if anything urgent comes up, then I will be reached.

Medium term planning: monthly and quarterly

Monthly planning for me takes place on a Thursday evening and I use the same familiar "BLUG" mnemonic / framework to walk through a monthly (p) review, as I think of it, reflecting on the month finished and previewing the month to come. While the FFP has this (p)review for each week and quarter, it does not instill a monthly (p)review; I add this in because I've been doing monthly reviews for over a decade, as taught by David Allen in GTD, specifically to reflect on smaller projects that might not meet size or importance criteria for a quarterly goal and yet take longer than just a week. Remember from the GTD section above that horizon 2 is spheres of responsibility, for monthly review, and most people have 4-7…professionally; you may double this if you add in your personal spheres of responsibility and taking both into account, these cover the main domains of life.

With that as a preamble, what I actually do is I fold the notes page (right hand side) of my FFP in half vertically to create two columns: at the top of the left column, I write the name of the month that is finishing and at the top of the right column I write the name of the month that is upcoming. In the margin on the far left, I now write the eight main domains of my life (where the idea of life domains is courtesy of Michael Hyatt in his outstanding book, *Living Forward*[30]), grouped by my standard three categories of Self, Relationships, Career, where the domains or spheres of Self include Physical, Emotional, Intellectual (or if you prefer, Body, Spirit, Mind); the domains / spheres of Relationships include Parental, Marital, Familial/Social (or if you prefer, you could list the individual names of your children, partner, family members and/or closest friends, as applicable); and the domain / sphere of Career includes Vocational and the adjacent Avocational (work you do for pay, and not; or, if you prefer, you could list the three or four main spheres of responsibility you have at work, such as CARE: Clinical Administrative Research and Education). Then under the month concluding, on the left, I write my biggest win in each domain. Under the month upcoming, on the right, I write my priority (most important unfinished business, something I need to prepare for, or something that I'm looking forward to doing) for each domain. Thus, the B and U of BLUG have been completed.

The above is expanded on the right-hand page (see Figure 2). I also then put a red asterisk next to my overall priorities for Self, Relationships and Career, and add them into ToDoIst, with a date I will do it and time estimate. For lessons learned each month, and what I'm grateful for in the month wrapping up, I write that in additional blank space on the left-hand page.

Quarterly planning for me ideally takes place off-site, where I define off-site realistically to mean just anywhere away from my home or my office (as opposed to idealistically, where a personal off-site retreat is again on that proverbial desert island). This idea comes again from *Essentialism*, in which McKeown recommends on day five of the Essentialism 21-day challenge, "Schedule a personal quarterly off-site to explore what is essential."[31] Having discussed *where* I do my quarterly planning, *when* do I do this? Typically in the last one or two weeks of the month preceding the next quarter; so for example, I will plan for the first quarter of the year (January, February, March), "Q1," in the last two weeks of December; I plan for the second quarter of the year (April, May, June), "Q2," in the last two weeks of March; I plan for the third quarter of the year (July, August, September), "Q3," in the last two weeks of June; and I plan for the fourth quarter of the year (October, November, December), "Q4," in the last two weeks of September. During my off-site (*where*), I (*who*) again use the Full

Focus Planner *(what)*, which guides one through a series of reflections similar to the weekly (p)review in that the questions posed help you to review the quarter wrapping up (biggest wins and how far you got on your Quarterly Big 3; what worked and what didn't) and preview the quarter coming up by writing about what you want to KISS (where KISS again stands for Keep Improve Start Stop); reviewing your annual goals (anything you want to revise or replace?) and selecting the two to three for the next quarter. Sometimes I save only two annual goals for the final quarter so that my Q4 (October 1-December 31) Relationship goal can be plan and deliver enjoyable and meaningful holidays (Halloween, Thanksgiving, Hanukkah / Christmas, New Year's) for my girls and my family beyond. Again, this fits well for a quarterly goal because it is something, given the scope of the goal articulated, that takes more than one month. This also makes the point that you may choose which annual goals to pursue in which quarter based on seasons, and or seasonal deadlines or responsibilities.

While the idea of quarterly planning may be new for some, it is well written about in the time management literature. As stated in an iGrad article, "The idea is that 90 days is a substantial enough time to make a change but not so long that it's overwhelming. Setting (quarterly) resolutions also allows you to set significantly more than you'd likely set as yearly resolutions,"[32]

Long term planning: annually and beyond

Annual planning for me takes place in the last two to three weeks of December; this is the *when*. In terms of *where*, pre-COVID-19, my favorite "off-site" location in which to do this was literally in the clouds, that is, on an airplane en route to or from winter vacation, sometimes to my mother-in-law in Australia, which takes fourteen hours from California, thus offering more than enough time to get things done, so to speak. *What* does my annual planning consist of? Quarterly planning *plus* ten to twelve annual goals, somewhat evenly spread across the three recurring categories of Self, Relationships and Career, where for me Self again includes Physical, Emotional, and Intellectual domains (or perhaps for others, mind-body-spirit); Relationships, which for me includes Parental, Marital, and Familial / Social; and Vocational and Avocational. Circling back to essentialism, I write down my priority for each domain. Then I follow my strategy for quarterly planning.

Annual planning in quarters is also beneficial, because whereas each of us may evolve a great deal over the course of 365 days in terms goals, there is less significant interval change from the beginning of the first quarter (Q1), for example, to the end in terms of top priorities. Not only you, but also the world may change a great deal in the course of the year as 2020 with COVID-19 has shown us all. Quarterly goals allow one to pivot to pursue redefined objectives should unknown circumstances arise. For example, the 2020 Q2 goals I thought about in December 2019 were very different from the ones I re-thought through when I got to the last two weeks of March 2020 (as COVID-19 hit) and focused on my quarterly planning for Q2.

Planning beyond the annual includes thinking about what you want to choose to pursue in the next three to five to ten years and beyond, with beyond including thinking about one's purpose in life. This may evolve over time and for many may have a spiritual or religious aspect, component or influence to it. If your reaction to the past two sentences includes something along the lines of "how can I find time to think about the meaning of life when I can barely find time to think about or plan for what's for dinner" then this comes full circle back to the purpose of this chapter, which is, that if you fail to plan, you are planning to fail, and the importance of having overlapping and intersecting planning resources like GTD (bottom's up approach), FFP (top down approach), and ToDoIst to pull it all together. For me, using this trifecta of an approach has enabled me to be able to think more about higher level issues, with less perseverating about what's for dinner.

Q&A: Planning

The following questions were written by radiologist Anna Trofimova, MD, PhD, in preparation for my October 15, 2020, AAWR webinar on Getting Things Done, 3rd in the Work/Life Balance Series for the year; the answers are what I prepared in advance to say.

> *Question 1.I enjoy learning about new productivity techniques but struggle with implementing them into my daily life: after a few weeks, the excitement about a new routine or technique is gone and I eventually give up. Do you have any advice regarding how to make these new changes last?*

Consider using a habits-tracking journal and try to cultivate the daily habit of planning or fifteen minutes of getting your backlogged tasks organized into ToDoIst. Next, recognize if you tend to prefer novelty over familiarity; other people are the opposite. If you fall into the former camp, then consider mixing up a routine or habit to keep it fresh (for example, working on exercising daily? Exercise daily, yet change up the type exercise, for example, mixing strength training with cardio instead of running every day). Finally, scheduling can also be very effective – for many, if it is on the calendar it happens, so consider scheduling a recurring weekly review of projects on your calendar, maybe for Thursday or Friday afternoon or some other not highly productive time, so it happens.

> *Question 2.Has the COVID-19 pandemic affected your*

approach to getting things done? Have you learned
something new?

In some ways no and some ways yes. No, in that whereas there have been some tweaks here and there, as is always the case as life circumstances including children and work evolve, still my fundamental methods not only didn't significantly change but also, I believe helped, help me to get through this unprecedented pandemic time with as much sanity and productivity as possible.

In other ways yes, COVID-19 has affected my approach to getting things done in that the pandemic has been a reminder about what is a priority—health, family and how we choose to spend our time — and a reminder to myself, in trying to get things done, to try to be kind and gentle to myself and take care of myself in terms of sleep and exercise, among other things, so I can best take of others.

[2022 addendum: It is times when life throws you the unexpected that it can be most helpful to lean in to and embrace regular planning and routine, because these provide stability in unstable times. For example, the week my first round of edits of this book were due, my 5-year-old got influenza A (despite the flu shot) and then four days later, my babysitter tested positive for COVID-19 (despite receiving the booster earlier in the fall) and had to quarantine, knocking out my regular childcare. I was able "keep calm and carry on" by leaning on my routines, as insurance that the essentials – and just the essentials – got done.]

Question 3. What do you think about procrastination and
ways to approach it?

What I think about procrastination is that we are all human and procrastination hits all of us at one point or another.

Ways to approach it are to 1) notice it, and 2) try to understand it, that is, try to recognize why you are you procrastinating.

Is it because it is not worth doing in the first place (in which case cross it off your list and stop feeling guilty) or is it because there is some associated emotional burden that you need to think through? For example: promotion — yes, it's a huge project to put together a promotion dossier and it needs to be broken down into smaller pieces, and yet are you also putting it off because of fear of failure or you don't think you're worthy? Depending on what you're procrastinating about, talk about it with a mentor or friend. Finally, I return to the frog: if you decide what you are procrastinating about is important and is a priority, then schedule it in, ideally as close to the beginning of a quarter, month, week or day as possible—with external accountability if needed—and then eat that frog first.

Question 4. I feel that for me the most difficult step is to start, and I often end up postponing working on the task until the last minute. Do you ever struggle with this and what helps you to overcome this resistance to start?

Absolutely. I think that all (or at least most of us) struggle with starting things and sometimes postpone a task until the last minute; this ties in with question three above about procrastination. Again, there is some psychology here, right? Knowing yourself is important. Do you work at a slow and steady clip, or in quick bursts of intense effort?

If you are the latter and you are doing good work, then keep it up and stop feeling bad about it; it's how you work. It is hard to change our natural tendencies, and yet if you want to work more like a marathoner, if it is a priority, then break down a task into manageable subtasks, schedule them in and hold yourself accountable in some way.

Question 5. I enjoyed learning about your productivity system; however, I'm concerned that my current list of backlogged tasks will prevent me from effective implementation of the steps you described. What can you recommend for those who are currently trying to catch up with the long list of pending items?

I hear you. We have all been there where we go through a particularly hectic period or haven't really ever been organized the way we would like to be, and it can leave you feeling overwhelmed and unable to deal with current tasks at hand.

To quote the popular Chinese proverb, "The best time to plant a tree was 20 years ago. The second best time is now." In other words, if you want to get through your current list of backlogged tasks, then the only way to get through them is to start now. Furthermore, as covered in Chapter 2, if you have 168 hours, you have more time than you think. If you decide getting organized and catching up is a priority, then break it down into manageable tasks, schedule them in and hold yourself accountable in some way. This is not going to be accomplished in a week, but maybe in a month or a quarter. If you can only read one book of those that I have recommended, then I would say when you are exercising, commuting, or doing mundane tasks around the house like laundry or dealing with the dishwasher, listen to David Allen's *Getting Things Done (GTD)*, collect everything in your inboxes and fifteen minutes a day, four-to-five days a week, work through it. Slowly but surely, you will catch up.

Conclusion

To plan effectively, you need a simple, flexible easy-to-use trusted system which you actually use on a regular (daily, weekly, monthly, quarterly, annual) basis. There are many organizational systems out there and each has its advantages and limitations and yet after much reading and research, my personal recommendations are for GTD by David Allen, the Full Focus Planner by Michael Hyatt, and the productivity app ToDoIst. The practical implications here are that anyone who is interested can use these resources at little to no cost to effectively plan in the short, medium, and long term.

At the same time, I do not want to close this chapter without the reminder to myself and others to be kind and gentle to and with yourself in terms of planning and getting things done. We only have one life to live so we need to enjoy the process, the getting there, not just the end result. Concluding along these existential lines about one life to live and time, I will close with this quotation from Laura Vanderkam: "Expectations are infinite. Time is finite. You are always choosing. Choose well." [33]

Once you have chosen well and planned, a logical next step is to keep in mind the importance of the pre-meeting meeting.

Figure 1. ToDoIst

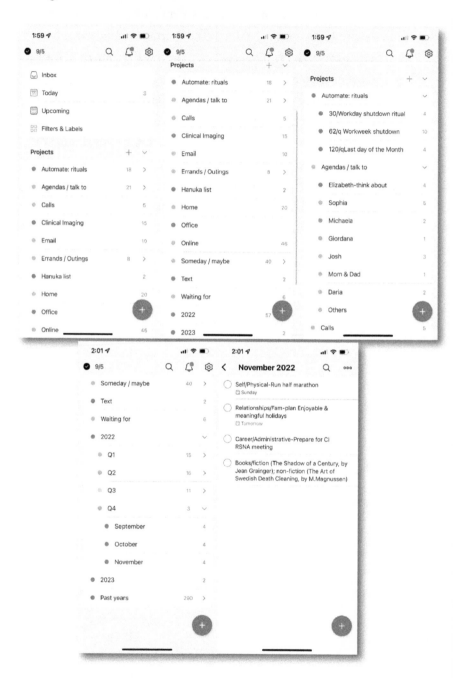

Figure 2. Monthly planning

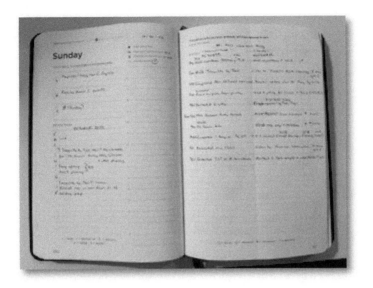

4

Remember the pre-meeting meeting...and that you are *not* an impostor

The hour in which I discovered the importance of the pre-meeting meeting was early—sometime between 7 and 8 a.m. while seated in front of weak coffee in a freezing hotel conference room. Yet the strong words I was listening to woke me up: I knew I was listening to a game-changer.

The conference was the annual meeting of the American College of Radiology (ACR), which takes place every spring in Washington, DC, unless a COVID-19 pandemic is taking place, in which case it is virtual. For many years now, on the Monday of the annual ACR conference, at 7 a.m., the American Association for Women in Radiology (AAWR) holds a Coffee and Muffins event with a speaker. The list of speakers in the past decade reads like a who's who of organized radiology, therefore when I became the President-elect of the AAWR in 2018, I changed the

name of the event to something I considered more fitting: Power Hour. The powerful words I was listening to in 2018 came from Cheri Canon, MD, Chair of the Department of Radiology at the University of Alabama at Birmingham and 2021 ACR Gold Medal winner—only the eleventh woman in the nearly one-hundred-year history of the ACR (the first woman being two-time Nobel Prize winner Marie Curie). The title of Dr. Canon's talk was intriguing and drew a crowd that made it standing room only: "Be Fearless....Or at least appear to be." As Dr. Canon stood at the front of the room, not behind the podium but rather poised and walking in front with flashcards in her hand which she referred to occasionally, she did appear to be fearless as she commanded the room.

The title of Dr. Canon's "Be Fearless" talk, she explained, arose from a conversation she had recently had with a male colleague at a meeting, who told her that she was absolutely fearless. "Dr. Canon felt it was an ironic statement," wrote Dr. Michelle Dorsey, in a post for the organization RADequal (formerly RADxx), an initiative co-founded by Dr. Geraldine McGinty and Ambra Health which promotes networking and mentorship opportunities for leaders in radiology and informatics. Why? Because, Dr. Canon relayed, not a day goes by that she doesn't feel fear. . .and that can be a good thing. Why? "The feeling of fear is an indicator that something is important and that it means something to you.... You can't be truly fearless, because as a leader people follow you, and you make decisions that affect their lives. It is appropriate to have a bit of fear about it as otherwise, it's just arrogance!"[34] wrote Dr. Dorsey, summarizing Dr. Canon's words for RadXX at the time.

I could completely relate to Dr. Canon's words—and maybe you can, too—because I think that I do sometimes/often use fear as a guide. Yet, the most important thing I took home from Dr. Canon's talk came slightly later when she talked about the importance of pre-meeting work: "Women should do the pre-work necessary to prepare" for important meetings, wrote Dr. Dorsey, summarizing Dr. Canon. "At board meetings, the decisions have frequently already been made before the meeting even starts. Men have pre-meetings, have discussed how they will vote, and know their talking points. Women approach board meetings differently as they prepare and bring data with the hopes that there will be a collective discussion and a group decision."[35] In other words, women should have pre-meetings too.

Overview of chapter lesson

The purpose of this chapter is to explore the importance of pre-meeting meetings. First, I define the pre-meeting meeting and then Impostor Syndrome, which can affect the success of meetings. Second, I will discuss what I had to overcome to take the first step in adopting the pre-meeting meeting and trying to abandon Impostor Syndrome. Third, I will talk through what I learned, and how the reader can avoid the mistakes I have made with specific ways to effectively prepare for pre-meeting meetings.

The pre-meeting meeting defined, and the related concept of Impostor Syndrome

A meeting is defined, according to the Oxford Dictionary, as an "occasion when people come together to discuss or decide something."[36] The preposition "pre" means "previous to" or "before." Therefore, the pre-meeting meeting is defined as when people come together to discuss or decide something *before* the main occasion when people come together to discuss or decide something. In other words, the decision-making process starts at the pre-meeting meeting. If you are not familiar with the term pre-meeting meeting, then you may have heard of the more common term "debriefing," which comes *after* a meeting and can involve discussing what went well, what could have been done differently, and next steps. In contrast, the pre-meeting meeting comes *before* a meeting and can involve discussing agenda items, especially potentially controversial issues. As the *Harvard Business Review* reports, "Pre-meetings are essential for anyone looking to have a successful meeting about a contentious issue. They are opportunities for information gathering, coalition building, building trust and rapport with allies and potential detractors, and stress testing and refining your arguments and perspectives. That way, by the time the actual meeting happens, you have a well-thought-out set of justifications for your point of view."[37]

Being effective at either meeting—the main event or the one before—requires, among other things, preparation and confidence. While the former may have specific obvious and or delineated steps, the latter may be less straight forward, especially for women. Why? Because of Impostor Syndrome, defined by Oxford Languages as "the persistent inability to believe that one's success is deserved or has been legitimately achieved as a result of one's own efforts or skills."[38] Although never an official diagnosis in the DSM (Diagnostic and Statistical Manual of mental disorders), Impostor Syndrome was initially described by psychologists in the 1970s as tending to occur among highly driven individuals who have difficulty genuinely believing in and owning their achievements, instead enduring self-doubt and anxiety that others will eventually uncover them as frauds because they believe—despite objective external evidence to the contrary – that their successes are somehow due to luck rather than to ability. If you've never heard of this term, the reason for it makes sense: many or most people with impostor syndrome feelings do not talk about it, because of fear of being found out.

In contrast to the hour in which I first learned about the pre-meeting meeting, which was very early in a freezing (conference) room, the hour in which I first learned about Impostor Syndrome was very late—sometime between 10:30-11:30 p.m.—and I was sweating through my hospital-issued scrubs. Yet again, though, the strong words I was listening to caught my attention and calmed me down: I knew then, too, that was listening to another game-changer and I wrote about it a 2021 *Clinical Imaging* article:

"Back in 2005–2006, when I was a junior radiology resident taking night call in the Emergency Department (ED) in the days before 24/7 attending coverage, I first learned of Impostor Syndrome from my mother, a clinical psychologist. In a panicked call from the ED late one night, in which I doubted my abilities despite all evidence from residency that I was competent, my mother helped me to calm down with a "name it to tame it" strategy. "You're defining and experiencing Impostor Syndrome," she explained, sharing that, "psychologists and others acknowledge that it is a very real and specific form of intellectual self-doubt [which] occurs among high achievers who are unable to internalize and accept their success…by definition, most people with impostor feelings suffer in silence".[1] Furthermore, the syndrome has long been documented as having a propensity to affect high-achieving women."[39]

Thus, part of my motivation for explicitly writing about Impostor Syndrome is so that it is not a silent topic for

high-achieving women, which may include many of the professional working mothers reading this book, as it does for me.

Adopting the pre-meeting meeting and (trying to) abandon Impostor Syndrome

The idea of the pre-meeting meeting is a pearl because once you
know about it, you understand that without having them yourself,
you risk letting other people make big decisions instead of con-
trolling the outcome as much as possible yourself. You can avoid
this and adopt the pre-meeting meeting as a professional habit by
intentionally pausing and asking yourself the following essentialist
question before going into your next important meeting: What is
the one thing I really want to achieve coming out of this meeting?
Or, slightly rephrased, What's the most important thing I need to
achieve with this meeting? Ask this question(s), and then work
backwards from this to achieve the desired outcome, setting up
pre-meeting meetings as needed.

Another way or framework in which to look at this lesson
is, again, through the journalistic lens I like to apply of the 5Ws
and an H: *Who* is the pre-meeting meeting relevant for? *What* is
it important for? *When* and *where* should it be utilized? *Why* is it
important? *How* do you implement it?

- **Who**: It is hard to think of any professional who
  would not benefit from using pre-meeting meetings
  before important meetings in their work.

- **What**: A principle is defined as a rule guiding one's
  behavior, and through this chapter I am striving to
  convey that the pre-meeting meeting should be a
  rule guiding work behavior for professional working

mothers to most effectively get things done in the office (whether it be a physical or virtual).

- **When**: The pre-meeting meeting should be applied whenever the meeting, or the outcome of a meeting, is important, where important is defined as having significance or value and likely to have a profound effect on success, survival, or well-being. "When" should also be sufficiently in advance of the main event to give people time to reflect about changing their minds, if need be.

- **Where**: Wherever pre-meeting work can most effectively get done, either virtually or in person at an office.

- **Why**: If you do not apply this principle, then again, you risk an important decision being made or determined by someone other than you.

- **How**: Consider the best modality, which could be phone, text, email, or even encrypted electronic communication. Sometimes, when discussing a sensitive matter, the best approach is off-line; when in doubt, pick up the telephone – while recorded lines exist, it is much easier for an email to be forward than a phone conversation to be shared, if confidentiality is a concern.

The opposite of adopt is to abandon, and from my own personal experience, I can say that abandoning Impostor Syndrome may be much harder than adopting the use of the pre-meeting meeting. For example, I first learned about Impostor Syndrome in 2005 as a junior radiology resident, and yet, as I wrote further in the 2021 *Clinical Imaging* piece,

"Fast forward 15 years: In February 2020, I officially became a full Professor of Radiology. By March, COVID-19 was an international pandemic with widespread shelter-in-place orders. By April, I was working remotely as the radiologist for several multi-disciplinary breast cancer tumor boards weekly. One morning in May when I logged on, I noticed for the first time that my division chief was present as well. I panicked and texted her, "It's making me nervous to see you on this conference. Did you get feedback they don't like how I'm doing? Please LMK so I can do better if that's the case!" I literally could *not* think of another explanation for why she was attending. A few minutes later she replied: "Not at all!!! Dr. A had mentioned wanting to discuss some data she had so I thought I should tune in." As I sighed with relief, I made the self-diagnosis: Impostor Syndrome. Still."

This experience is not uncommon. Speaking in London for her *Becoming* book tour, former first lady Michelle Obama—who wrote about Impostor Syndrome in her book as well—spoke about how Imposter Syndrome continues to impact her life today. "It never goes away," she said. "It's sort of like 'you're actually listening to me?' It doesn't go away, that feeling of 'I don't know if the world should take me seriously; I'm just Michelle Robinson, that little girl on the south side who went to public school'."[40] Impostor Syndrome is not unique to medicine or politics. Even in the world of acting, Golden Globe Award and

Academy Award winner Natalie Portman has said, speaking at a 2015 event at her alma mater, Harvard, how she never felt like she deserved to be at the university during her time there. "Today I feel much like I did when I came to Harvard Yard as a freshman in 1999," she told the students who had gathered to listen to her. "I felt like there had been some mistake, that I wasn't smart enough to be in this company, and that every time I opened my mouth I would have to prove that I wasn't just a dumb actress."[41] Even Sheryl Sandberg, ranked 11th on the Forbes Power Women List and 12th place on America's Self-Made Women in 2018, wrote about feeling that she had managed to "fool everyone yet again, and one day she would be caught."[42] If you, too, feel this way sometimes, then what can you do about it?

Best practices

In order to practice the pre-meeting meeting, build the habit of using this principle by looking at upcoming meetings on your calendar and asking yourself, "What is the one thing or the most important thing I want to achieve coming out of this meeting?" Identify what this is, and if there is an important decision potentially to be made—where important is defined again as having great significance or value with the likelihood of having profound effect on the success or well-being or yourself or others—then work backwards from the desired outcome by speaking, emailing, or texting beforehand with those who have the potential to influence the discussion and decision. Before you do so, know your talking points clearly.

This strategy, which I highly recommend, is supported by the literature. For example, in his book, *Leadership Gold*, John Maxwell recounts the advice of a mentor who told him to ascertain who key influencers were going to be in a meeting and meet with them beforehand. Maxwell and others use the phrase "the meeting before the meeting," but they are referring to the same process advocated for by Dr. Canon, one "of checking in with key players prior to the larger meeting—gaining their buy-in, develop trust, and avoid being blindsided later on."[43]

This begs the question: how do you prepare for a pre-meeting meeting? Seriously. As seriously as you would or will for the main meeting. The goal of each pre-meeting meeting—and there may be several depending on the size of the main event—is to try to line up each person as your advocate before the main event happens. Listen, non-defensively, and really hear all concerns and objections they may have, and as recommended by Maxwell, consider the following questions to pose to your potential advocates about your idea: Does this idea make sense to you? Align with initiatives in your area? Do you agree with it? If yes, then would you back me up when I present it at the meeting? If not, why not? (far better to know this in advance, when you still might have a chance to turn things around before the main event).

After having pre-meeting meetings, you may not have enlisted 100 percent of key decision-makers as advocates. But, by pre-selling your ideas before the big meeting, you will at least know who your supporters are, who is neutral, and who is downright opposed—and be better able to respectfully address all points of view in the main meeting. Someone may also raise a legitimate concern you hadn't thought of which can be fixed in advance and thus removed as a problem from the table at the main meeting. In this way, you are doing the opposite of "if you fail to plan, you are planning to fail." Rather, you are planning — planning for success.

What about trying to abandon Impostor Syndrome? First, acknowledge that it may not be possible to eradicate it completely. Second, consider the "5Rs for tackling Impostor Syndrome (IS)" developed by interventional radiologist Dr. Gloria Salazar from her individual experiences, as shared in the same co-authored 2021 *Clinical Imaging* paper previously mentioned in this chapter:

1. **"Recognize it first**: Acknowledging that you are experiencing IS is the first step towards managing it. Reconcile your feelings by asking the following questions: What is prompting the IS? How does it make me feel? Why is this happening now?

2. **Rational thinking**: Collect evidence from your achievements and understand the rationale behind being invited to be a panelist/keynote speaker or to be offered a position of leadership, for example. You may think you are not qualified and/or that there are other physicians more qualified than you. Think to yourself: "I am invited to give this talk. I have worked for 10 years in this field of expertise; there were other obvious candidates that are as qualified as me, however, the scientific committee choose me for a reason." Another approach is to ask a mentor or someone who genuinely cares about your career if you are ready and qualified for the challenges that a specific leadership position brings.

3. **Reframe**: Understand what a specific opportunity means to your career and your values. In the case of a presentation, think about what values/experiences you bring to the audience. In the case of leadership position, understand what is preventing you from pursuing that role. Imagine yourself in that position and how you feel about it.

4. **Ready**: Now that you have reframed your thinking, let go of the negative feelings and focus on the prize. As mentioned by Jessica Bennett in her book *Feminist Fight Club*, many female leaders overprepare to avoid feeling like an imposter.

5. **Repeat if recurrent**: Unfortunately, Impostor Syndrome is likely to repeat itself, particularly when you are faced with challenges, so be ready to repeat the "5 R s" whenever you need it."[44]

There are limitations to the "pre-meeting meeting" pearl. First, the efficacy of pre-meeting meetings may vary according to where on the spectrum from introversion to extroversion an individual stands. For example, in one study of 252 working adults, it was found "that the relationship between pre-meeting talk and perceived meeting effectiveness was stronger for less extraverted participants."[45] Second, having a pre-meeting meeting does not always ensure that the actual meeting outcome will go the way you want. Nevertheless, when an outcome is important, remembering to have a pre-meeting meeting will ensure that you've done everything you could to facilitate the desired outcome.

Conclusion

The purpose of this chapter was to explore the importance of pre-meeting meetings and of Impostor Syndrome. The principal findings are that as a professional working mother, do not be naive about bringing data alone to a meeting with the hopes that there will be a collective discussion and group decision; men have pre-meetings, presenting talking points and how votes might be cast, and women should too. Furthermore, if you experience Impostor Syndrome, you are not alone and there are ways to tackle it. However, in both leading meetings and pre-meeting meetings, as well as trying to combat Impostor Syndrome, the wisdom of Voltaire as discussed in the next chapter is deeply relevant as well: Don't let the perfect be the enemy of the good.

5

Don't let the perfect
be the enemy of the good

"Do not let the perfect be the enemy of the good."
—Voltaire

There is not one moment in which I discovered this lesson, nor can I recall when I first learned of the quotation above. And yet it is such an important one that the quotation hangs on my home office wall near Mark Twain's "Eat Your Frog." I do not have it hanging in my professional office, because as a recovering perfectionist, so to speak, my clinical work is the last sphere in which I continue to strive for perfection, or as close to perfection as humanly possible, when taking care of my patients. In other spheres, however, I try to follow Voltaire's sage advice and instead try to be a satisficer, a term used to describe people whose choices derive from reasonable or modest criteria rather than a drive for perfection.

Overview of this chapter lesson
First, I will provide a focused review of literature on the topic of

not letting the perfect be the enemy of the good. Second, through examples of not heeding the call, I will illuminate what happens when you do not apply this principle. Third, six steps to heed the principle "don't let the perfect be the enemy of the good" will be presented.

What does the literature have to say about "Don't let the perfect be the enemy of the good?"

Original Source

According to the Concise Oxford Dictionary of Quotations, "Perfect is the enemy of the good" is a saying which is commonly attributed to Voltaire, who quoted an Italian proverb in his *Dictionnaire philosophique* in 1770: *Il meglio è l'inimico del bene.* As a fluent Italian speaker, thanks to a year in Rome before medical school where I supported myself teaching English, it sparks joy for me to provide my own direct translation: "The better is the enemy of the good." To dissect this further, it surprised me, given the current quotation (don't let the *perfect* be the enemy of the good), that the original Italian did not read "Il migliore" (the best) or "il perfetto" (perfect) è l'inimico del bene (is the enemy of the good). This suggests to me that it has evolved over time, possibly as more unrealistic standards have insidiously crept into society, from good to better, better to best, and from best to perfect.

Good-better-best-perfect. If the "Il meglio" ("the better") sentence was written in 1770 and by 2022 (at the time of editing) we are now at the perfect, so to speak, then in sum, we seem to have gone from better (1770)—best (1896, the halfway point)—perfect (2022). In other words, we seem to have evolved from "Il meglio è l'inimico del bene," "the better is the enemy of the well" or good to "the best is the enemy of the good" and finally "the perfect is the enemy of the good," over the course of 252 years. Moreover, approximately every 125 years, or every one to two generations, the bar appears to be getting raised. For example, my father, age 89 at the time of this writing, is a child of two Italian immigrants. By what standards was he brought up? Was he urged to be perfect, or rather to do his best? Or was good, well, good enough? "There was no external emphasis on perfection," my Dad said during a conversation while I was writing the manuscript for this book, "The drive, as a as a first-generation child, was to strive to do *better*, make thing *better* for the next generation, as my parents had done for me and my brother and sister by their very act of coming to this country."[46] Better. *Meglio, non perfetto.*

Now I'm not saying striving for improvement is a bad thing; growth is a critical element for happiness, and as the child of immigrants, my Dad (and my mother too) was born and raised in an environment of, we (his parents) left Italy for a better (better, not best or perfect) life; and the life that they created in Brooklyn, New York—in contrast to Southern Italy at the beginning of the twentieth century—was good. And they hoped for their children that it would be better; and my father hoped for his children the best. However, I think the important points to keep in mind are that, perfection is not humanly possible and constantly striving for the best – while important in certain arenas – is not only exhausting but also may result in diminishing marginal returns.

I am a big proponent of the idea that words matter. For example, professionally, in radiology, we dictate all our reports, describing the findings, our impression and management recommendation for the imaging studies we interpret, and for phrases that I use repeatedly, I take the time to think intentionally about the words I want to use to convey what I want to say, whatever it is, and then save the verbiage so that I can insert it exactly as is whenever I want to; more on the value of automating what you can in Chapter 1, related to preventing decision fatigue. Moreover, personally as a mother, I became increasingly aware of just how often "perfect" peppers my speech and the speech of the people around me, including unfortunately, my girls, ages five, eleven and fourteen at the time of this writing. Going forward, just as I have asked them to call me on apologizing too much (see Chapter 6), I have also asked them to call me on using the word "perfect," because I do not want the use of the word to pervade or intrude upon our unconscious and set up unrealistic, and quite frankly, unhelpful, or harmful standards. Choice of words is very important.

Forbes

More recently than Voltaire, and in a completely different industry, General George Patton once said, "A good plan today is better than a perfect one tomorrow."[47] Why is that? As a 2014 *Forbes* article explains, "Many entrepreneurs start their company wanting to build the perfect product or service for their customer. This is a big mistake and here is why: perfect can take too long to develop. Most entrepreneurs have a limited amount of development funds before they need to get paying customers."[48] I believe that this is relevant for individuals as well. Specifically, many professional working women – and I'm speaking from personal experience here — start out whatever they are doing with the intention for it to be perfect. And yet for individuals as well as companies, this is a big mistake because perfect takes too long and most people have limited time before they need to move on to something else – everything is an opportunity cost or tradeoff. By way of illustration, professionally, it is critical that I proofread my dictated reports to insure that the size and site of the breast cancer I'm describing, for example, is accurate, and yet after that? My goal is not noble-prize winning literature, rather a medically accurate and clinically impactful report. Reading over my report a second and third time is, at that point, an opportunity cost, potentially trading off minor stylistic changes for what is more important – spending that time compassionately speaking or just being with the patient in question, supporting her at what may be the beginning of a life-changing journey and I have the opportunity to frame it in as a positive and supportive a light as is reasonable.

A related idea is the Pareto principle, named for the Italian economist Vilfredo Pareto, which dictates that it takes 20 percent of the time to complete 80 percent of a task and that the last 20 percent of a task takes 80 percent of the effort. These diminishing returns in many cases do not make sense, continues the *Forbes* article, "Why Good is Better Than Perfect," relating an even more recent summarization or related idea, coined by Sheryl Sandberg: Done is better than perfect. As *Forbes* explains of this Sandberg quotation, "This does not mean doing a mediocre job or producing a poor-quality product. Being done and finishing a task gives every (business) person an outcome. This result will give them important success or failure metrics to decide what their next step will be." [49] My dictation example in the previous paragraph is illustrative, in that the diminishing returns (from re-reading a dictated report a second or third time) do not make sense, in terms of patient outcome.

Anxiety, depression, and decreased happiness are three more reasons why pursuing perfection does not make sense. "Satisficers are those who make a decision or take action once their criteria are met. That doesn't mean they'll settle for mediocrity; their criteria can be very high," writes author Gretchen Rubin. "Maximizers want to make the optimal decision...they can't make a decision until after they've examined every option, to make the best possible choice." And yet studies suggest satisficers are happier than maximizers, because while the latter expend more time and effort to come to a decision, they still feel anxious about whether the decision was the best one. Fear Of Missing Out (FOMO) is applicable not only to events but also to choices - fear of missing out on that which you didn't decide on or choose - and experiencing FOMO has been linking with depression.[50] In a world of seemingly infinite choices, there is probably not one best choice, but many. There is probably more than one choice out there that you would be happy with, so as my mother repeatedly said to me growing up, "make a decision, and stick to it!"

Harvard Business Review

The *Harvard Business Review* (HBR) has also written about this important topic of "don't let the perfect be the enemy of the good." A 2020 article published on Valentine's Day with the same title as the saying states: "We should all strive to do our best, but if you always aim for perfection, you may blow deadlines, annoy your colleagues, and miss out on opportunities…. [also] consider how perfectionism impacts your relationships. Are you setting unrealistic standards for those around you? The need to have it "perfect" will often annoy others, and in extreme cases, drive them away. For their sake — and yours — learn to be satisfied with good enough."[51] In other words, in all three categories (as discussed in Chapter 3 on planning) – Self, Relationships, Career – striving for perfect is not helpful.

To counteract perfectionistic tendencies, *Forbes* suggests experimenting in a small stakes setting with relaxing your standards and seeing what happens – what, if anything, negative occurs? As a clinician-scientist, this proposed experiment appealed to me, because I would be (informally) collecting personal data, if you will, and then letting the results (hopefully) speak for themselves that striving for perfection is neither helpful nor necessary. So, I tried this with a PowerPoint for a low stake's presentation: I made the decision to set a timer for sixty minutes and stick to it, and when then timer went off, I spell checked the presentation and sent to the more senior person who had booked me. "This is great!" she replied less than an hour later, when I would otherwise still have been working on the presentation. Immediate feedback that in certain, arguably many circumstances, relaxing my standards slightly made no difference to the outcome—except I had extra time to use intentionally and otherwise. What upcoming low stakes setting could you experiment with in terms of relaxing your standards and seeing what happens? What, if anything, negative happened? If nothing, then let this help you too live out not letting the perfect be the enemy of the good.

Alluded to indirectly in the above HBR account is the alternative to perfection of satisficing, defined as follows: "Satisficing is a decision-making strategy or cognitive heuristic that entails searching through the available alternatives until an acceptability threshold is met. The term *satisficing*, a portmanteau of *satisfy* and *suffice*, was introduced by Herbert A. Simon in 1956, although the concept was first posted in his 1947 book *Administrative Behavior*."[52] So although satisficing may be a new concept for many professional mothers – it certainly was for me when I first came across it – as an idea, it is actually three-quarters of a century old. A related, but relatively more recent, idea is that of the "nirvana fallacy," defined as the misconception of comparing actual things with idealized alternative options or the inclination to think that there is a perfect way of solving a problem; this idea was named by economist Harold Demsetz in 1969.[53] Finally, the "perfect solution fallacy" creates a false dichotomy pitting a realistic achievable option against another idealized but unrealistic one; in this way, any alternative options are attackable because they are not perfect and thus fall short. What the nirvana and perfect solution fallacies, as well as maximizing (instead of satisficing), all have in common is letting the unobtainable perfect be the enemy of the obtainable good.

In sum, there are many reasons to heed Voltaire, Patton, Pareto, Sandberg, Rubin, and Simon, and in the next section we will explore what happens when one does not.

Examples of *not* heeding the call of Voltaire, Patton, Pareto, Sandberg, Rubin, and Simon — and what it costs

A college freshman with perfectionist tendencies. An English class assignment due Monday at 8 a.m. Paper done by Monday at 8 a.m. but not turned in until 8 p.m., because she kept going over and over it to try to make it perfect. Grade received on work: 100; grade received on paper: 50, due to being twelve hours late. What it cost her: 50 percent of her grade.

Another example. The college freshman is now a professional woman, still with perfectionist tendencies. An email needs to go out to the team she is leading. The earlier the email goes out, the better, because it is about confirming dates of availability. Email drafted by Friday at 5 p.m. but not sent until Monday mid-day because she kept proofreading it. Result: several team members no longer available, and now she must find others for the job. What it cost her: time and energy, that could have been used elsewhere.

Another example. The same professional woman is now a mother, too. She has a hard stop at 5 p.m. so she can get home by 5:30 p.m. to relieve the babysitter and spend time with her baby before she goes to sleep. Urgent email now goes out at 4:55 p.m. Done is better than perfect. Reward: two hours with her reason for living.

Does any of the above bring to mind examples from your own academic, professional and motherhood journey?

During my own undergraduate academic experience, I majored in a program at Yale called Ethics, Politics and Economics (EP&E), and it was in a required course for the latter, one taught by Nobel prize-winning Professor William Nordhaus, that I remember learning about diminishing marginal returns (DMR) in quite an illustrative manner. I remember a classmate called out of the audience, having put up his hand affirmatively that he liked bananas, and watching the concept of DMR be played out on stage. The professor had the student take one bite of a yellow ripe banana, describe the experience, and then take another and another and another and another well into the second and possibly into the third banana. The first bite was delicious and so was the second, but at a certain point there was diminishing returns in terms of pleasure of eating more of that banana. Furthermore, as the stomach filled up during our late morning lecture, there was less room in the stomach for lunch choices ahead. Everything has a tradeoff, as Professor Nordhaus and his fruit demonstrated. Yet it was not until I had my first baby over a decade later, just before the beginning of my final year of diagnostic radiology residency when I was also studying for the oral boards to become a board-certified radiologist, that I acutely internally learned the idea of opportunity costs and trade-offs. Until Sophia was born, I could study an infinite number of hours to assuage my perfectionist tendencies and address impostor syndrome feelings by over preparing. But before Sophia, the opportunity cost was also never a deal breaker, giving up time with my purpose in life.

Sometimes it is a lifetime of overpreparation and perfectionism – commonly seem in those battling Impostor Syndrome – that is not checked until a child with compelling needs puts in perspective what is most important in life. This, in some ways, is the crux of it. You can let perfect be the enemy of the good, and yet as Laura Vanderkam wrote poignantly in her 2019 fable *Juliet's School of Possibilities,* "Expectations are infinite. Time is finite. You are always choosing. Choose well."[54]

Steps in heeding the principle don't let the perfect be the enemy of the good

For me, the following have been helpful in striving not to let the perfect be the enemy of the good:

1. Strive to be a satisficer: decide on criteria (for example, Mexican restaurant, outdoor dining, one mile radius from home, good margaritas,) and when the criteria are achieved, then make the selection and move on; ask what the minimal viable product is, such as dinner on the table, and then enjoy it when you remind yourself that done is better than perfect.

2. Check your work...a finite number of times. If you need to, follow a checklist and once each step is done, then you are done.

3. Post on office wall "don't let the perfect be the enemy of the good" or in kitchen (or anywhere else where it would be helpful to you) "done is better than perfect."

4. When I hear "perfect" coming out of my mouth or the mouths of my daughters, see if another word

—such as great or well done—can be substituted so as not to set up unrealistic expectations.

5. SMART: Before starting a project or reaching for a goal, however small (dinner) or big (this book), ask if it is SMART, as in Specific, Measurable, Achievable (or Attainable), Relevant, and Time-bound.

6. Make a deadline and stick to it. This is a paraphrase of my mother's "make a decision and stick to it!" In this case, the decision I'm committing to is a hard deadline, because a soft or moveable one encourages perfectionistic tendencies, whereas a hard or immovable one promotes a healthier approach.

The last on this list, setting deadlines and sticking to them, is particularly important for professional women because of Parkinson's law, which states that "work expands so as to fill the time available for its completion." You may be familiar with this phenomenon when packing a suitcase - maybe you have heard the advice to always choose a carry-on bag because wherever you are going, what you are packing will expand to fill the space available. Knowing Parkinson's law, you can choose the opposite, or Horstman's corollary to Parkinson's law, that work contracts to fit in the time we give it. Setting deadlines and sticking to them is one way of setting and respecting boundaries, which can be particularly helpful for recovering perfectionists – you can always channel your perfectionist tendencies towards perfection in observing the deadlines and boundaries you set for yourself.

Finally, if all else fails, try to heed "don't let the perfect be the enemy of the good" by returning to the essentialist focus of what the most important thing is that I need to do now or today, tomorrow, this week, this month, this quarter, this year, and or beyond. Consider your core values and what is more important. Having already proofed your email or report several times, is it more important that you proofread it one more time towards getting it as close to perfect as possible—or is done is better than perfect, and then you can submit it, go home and spend time with your children while they are still young and in the house?

Conclusion

The purpose of this chapter is to convey the importance of the "don't let the perfect be the enemy of the good" credo and the related principal findings that not genuinely adopting and living out this principle can lead to anxiety and depression, lack of productivity and happiness. The pearl is not without limitations and difficulties. For example, in patient care, again, I still strive for as close to perfection as humanly possible. Furthermore, to not only survive but also to thrive as a working mother in both the personal and professional spheres of our lives, while we must genuinely say good-bye to the pursuit of perfection, doing so after years of perfectionistic tendencies can be challenging to course correct. Another related challenge: stop over-apologizing unnecessarily – the topic of the following chapter.

6

Stop over-apologizing

It was a eureka moment courtesy of Dr. Hedvig Hricak, one of the most famous and influential women in radiology—ever. Years later, I still remember her most important point: Stop over-apologizing.

The setting was a gathering of the Mentorship Program for Women in Radiology, a program I founded at my institution when I was a Women's Imaging fellow in 2009/2010. The program, still going strong over a decade later, aims to provide intimate gatherings over wine and cheese for interested radiologists, radiologists in training and medical students considering the specialty to hear the inspiring stories of successful women in radiology—the more personal side. I started the program because *I* wanted to hear from these women; I wanted to know when I was starting out my career, how did *she* do it? At that evening circa 2011 or 2012, the speaker was Dr. Hricak, the formidable Chair of the Department of Radiology at Memorial Sloan Kettering Cancer Center (MSKCC) in New York City from 1999-2023, remarkable in any specialty but particularly so in radiology where the percentage of women practicing radiology is still only approximately 25 percent,

according to a 2019 American College of Radiology (ACR) Commission on Human Resources (HR) workforce survey,[55] and the percentage of female chairs of radiology departments is at a high of (drumroll) 17 percent.[56]

Dr. Hricak is the height of European elegance and decorum, at the same time that she is omnipotent and formidable. She described how, in her capacity as chair of the department, men and women come into her office to ask for things such as a promotion, a raise, or time off. She noticed over time that women often begin by apologizing for no reason whatsoever, whereas men did not. She affirmed the importance of apologizing when appropriate and yet watching your language so that you as a professional woman do not do so unnecessarily.

At that moment, I started listening to myself more carefully and I saw just how right Dr. Hricak was. "I'm sorry" peppered so much of the speech coming out of my mouth that I was appalled. To hold myself accountable and try to not pass on this unhelpful trait to the next generation, I have asked my daughters to call me out on it when I say "I'm sorry" unnecessarily.

Do you say a lot of "I'm sorry" too, even when it might not be indicated?

Overview of chapter lesson

Let's explore why we, as professional working mothers, tend to apologize too often or when there is no actual reason to do so. First, the topic will be explored in a point-counter point style discussion. Second, the psychology of apologizing will be considered. Third, you will find specific practices to utilize to overcome over-apologizing.

Stop over-apologizing: point and counterpoint

When I started to think about writing this book, I began by making a list of lessons learned (starting with eat your frog) to see if I had enough material. Dr. Hricak's point about women over-apologizing easily came out without much searching as a key point I have acquired, if not entirely mastered. With it in mind, I was curious what my husband would think about the issue, as I have learned a great deal from him in the two decades we have known each other, as his point of view as an extroverted attorney from outside the United States is often very different from mine as a relatively introverted radiologist born and raised in New York. From there, I posed the question to others in my personal and professional circles to gather a variety of perspectives.

Personal perspective #1: My spouse
Joshua Thompson, Esq., b. Sydney, Australia

> "It is comparatively normal in other English-speaking countries, other than the United States, to apologize more frequently and sincerely. While women should be cautious not to over-apologize, arguably the larger problems arise from the cultural norm in the United States that men apologize far too infrequently and, if they do, it is often defensively and lacking elements of sincere contrition, relative to men (and women) in other parts of the world."

Personal perspective #2: My mother-in-law
Elaine Thompson, PhD, Professor (Emerita) of
American and Australian Politics, University of
New South Wales, Sydney, Australia

"To be annoying, I think you are both right. Americans generally (male and female) have a much more direct speech pattern than people in the UK Australia etc. So, to us outsiders, it often sounds rude and abrasive. It occurs in American children as well. The 'I want' or 'Give me' are much more common rather than, 'I'm sorry to interrupt but please pass the salt' style of talking.

However, the 'English' form because it contains words such as 'I'm sorry' or 'Excuse me' is not actually more polite or more thoughtful—indeed can hide extreme rudeness within apparently modest sounding speech.

All that having been said, women do have utterly different speech patterns to men and are not listened to even when they manage to get to say something. As a result, women use devices such as 'I'm sorry' to be able to break into discussions when they are simply being ignored or 'rolled over.' The alternative is to use male speech and be seen as an aggressive b-tch (instead of an assertive person) or overly opinionated etc. It's a difficult balancing act.

I suppose we have to develop devices (and there must be books about this now) to prevent the 'approval seeking' behavior of which the 'I'm sorry' is a part; another part is the rising inflection at the end of sentences.

I use to try to do what I do in my writing and that is to edit out all the 'I want to say,' 'I would like to say,' 'I think,' or 'In my opinion' or 'I'm sorry but' and say what you mean to say. You are not going to change the male culture to be more considerate in linguistic style so the best we can do is to speak with clarity and directness. All the 'I want' etc. phrases are just 'fillers' in any case and undercut the message.

Having said all that, if by using 'I'm sorry' you manage to break into the discussion and you are then able to say your piece, it's far better than being ignored!

Perhaps I am not the best person with whom to discuss this, as I have always been told that I am very direct and have no sense of 'diplomacy'—I say what I mean. To which I have always replied: if you think I'm direct, you should have met my mother!

Also… it's very easy to develop bad speech habits without being aware of them e.g., the use of 'like' as a filler which lots of young girls do; or 'um' etc. I suspect 'I'm sorry' may well be another one. So don't beat yourself up too badly!"

Personal perspective #3: MY mother
Lillian S. Kagan, PhD, (retired) clinical psychologist, b. Queens, NY

"I agree with Dr. Hricak. Girls and women have been groomed from a very young age to say I'm sorry, almost as easily and along with please and thank you. So, it's not that it's a natural biological difference between girls and boys, men and women, it's about nurture. Yes, boys are taught to say please, thank you and I'm sorry; but with girls it's at another level, where they are also groomed to be more accommodating, whereas in contrast boys to be more entitled. Saying I'm sorry is a part of that, along with being accommodating of others often ahead of oneself, thus putting oneself on the backburner, which can have profound and divergent effects in the professional sphere."

With that, it was time to take the question to my professional sphere—including back to Dr. Hricak herself, who along with Dr. Geraldine McGinty, had graciously hosted a small dinner in honor of my promotion to full Professor of Radiology in early March 2020. It was one week before the COVID-19 crisis hit New York City in full force. The dinner, one I will never forget for the company, conversation and views of the city, was like a last supper of our own. Afterwards, Geraldine sent a photo taken by the waiter of the happy table to the group and in the ensuing months, we had a series of email exchanges on topics ranging from the serious (impact of COVID-19 on professional woman) to the more mundane (what Netflix series to watch during shelter-in-place). So, I reopened the thread with the question: Do women apologize unnecessarily? Here's what this power table had to say, in order of emails received.

Professional perspective #1: Silvia Chiara Formenti MD, Professor and Chair, Department of Radiation Oncology, Weill Cornell Medicine, born in Milan and grew up in Italy

"What an interesting debate. My husband is British and apologizes all the time ("sorry to ask you to stop here" to the cab driver, "sorry for asking," to a police officer etc., etc.) . . . I think we need to distinguish the "politeness" of apology (common in UK, Australia, New Zealand, etc.) from the need to apologize when asking for recognition or professional support. Really different settings."

Professional perspective #2: Katia Dodelzon MD, Associate Professor of Clinical Radiology and Vice Chair of Clinical Operations for Radiology at Weill Cornell Medicine, born in Azerbaijan and also gre up in Israel

"I agree with Silvia. Two points:

1. Having lived in two relatively polar opposite cultures from a formality and granting respect/apologizing perspective prior to the US, I do not feel that the males in this country do not apologize enough/not polite enough rather it's a happy medium between the other two countries I've experienced.

2. It's not that women apologize too much; it is when they do. Predicating an ask for something they have earned professionally with a "I'm so sorry to bother you" or a "I'm so sorry to ask. . ." perpetuates the long-held idea that women are not as qualified (it's a reach/they cannot handle the position or the pressure and worst of all—they are not sure they even deserve what they are about to ask for). From a psychological point of view, you are priming the one being asked not to grant you what you are asking for. That is the problem. It's along similar lines to men applying for jobs they are not nearly qualified for and women holding back applying because they do not believe all their accolades and accomplishments are enough to warrant an application.

Sub point: I do it all the time still.

Will try to work on it inspired by Elizabeth—in the very least for my daughter's sake."

Professional perspective #3: Hedvig Hricak MD, PhD, Chair of the Department of Radiology, Memorial Sloan Kettering Cancer Center, born in Zagreb and grew up in Croatia

"Dear All, Hope, soon we can get together and continue our discussion in person.

Katia's points are perfect:

It's not that women apologize too much; it is <u>when they</u> <u>do</u>. . . More when we see each other."

Professional perspective #4: Geraldine McGinty, MD, MBA, Senior Associate Dean for Clinical Affairs, Professor of Clinical Radiology and Population Health Sciences at Weill Cornell Medicine, first female Chair of the American College of Radiology (ACR) Board of Chancellors in its nearly 100-year history, born and grew up in the UK, including Ireland

"Maybe it's my Irish resentment at 700 years of colonization but I love this on the British propensity for saying sorry: 'The readiness of the English to apologise for something they haven't done is remarkable, and it is matched by an unwillingness to apologise for what they have done.'

A lot of this comes back to the way women are socialized to think that we mustn't take up space. Glad that Katia and Elizabeth's daughters are being given a strong message to the contrary."

Professional perspective #5: Anna Starikov MD, (at the time) 4th year Diagnostic Radiology resident, New York-Presbyterian / Weill Cornell Medical Center, born in New York

"Yes, I am definitely guilty of apologizing too much. But hoping that thanks to you all and other strong intelligent women, the new generation (including our daughters) are more aware of this and thus able to claim what they have earned without hesitation or feeling like they need to downplay their achievements."

This begs the question: How *do* we give our daughters, and ourselves, this strong message, especially when women and girls are socialized to the contrary?

The Psychology of Apologizing: formative years

Regarding socialization of girls and apologizing, here is what the Child Mind Institute in New York City has to say: "A girl who is assertive might be called bossy, a girl who shows confidence in her ideas, conceited. Though still told to work hard, get ahead, and be successful, girls are often shamed… if they appear pushy, overly confident, or too forward," says the affiliated Dr. Busman.[57] As a result, starting at even a young age, girls begin to qualify their language by using softer statements (e.g., "I know" becomes "I'm not sure but") and apologies ("Sorry, would it be okay if I asked a question?"). Although these verbiage changes may be subtle, just consider the impact on one's overall developing self-esteem and confidence. Not good.

Tuning into word choice — such as "better" instead of "perfect" — is the first step to helping our daughters and ourselves use more confident language and mitigate over-apologizing and hedging. Both are problematic personally and professionally for girls and women. Over-apologizing is troublesome, especially starting sentences with "I'm sorry," because in this way the female is making a bad start at something from the get-go: "Beginning a comment with an apology immediately puts her in a one-down position…It instantly delegitimizes any authority she has," further explains Dr. Busman.[58] More subtle is hedging, with non-confident word choices including excuse me, can I ask, I might be wrong but, I don't know but. Again, this is problematic because lack of confidence personally can be a source of insecurity and unhappiness; professionally, it can mean the difference between advancement or not. In other words, over-apologizing can be costly in all spheres of your life. So how can we try to stop? How can we break this bad habit?

Overcoming over-apologizing

A contemporary expert in the field of habits is Charles Duhigg, *The New York Times* reporter and best-selling author of *The Power of Habit: What we do in life and business.* Backed by an extensive analysis of the science of habits, Duhigg explains, "The right way to think about breaking a habit is to think about changing that habit, and to do so, one needs to figure out the habit loop. According to scientific research, every habit consists of the three-part loop: a cue, a routine, and a reward."[59] Thus, to end a bad habit, identify the cue; determine the desired reward, then modify the routine. Could this framework be applied to the bad habit of over-apologizing? Is it applicable? If we tried to apply this framework to breaking the habit of over-apologizing, then what might that look like?

First, to identify the cue, start by noticing the associated location, time, emotional state, surroundings, and action. For example, does your over-apologizing occur more at home or at work? If at work, what time? All meetings or more likely to occur at late afternoon meetings when you are already worn out or stressed out (emotional state) by the day? Are the surroundings a familiar boardroom or does over-apologizing happen more often when you go to a new office for an important meeting? What is the cue or cues that trigger the action of over-apologizing? To make these identifications, you need to watch your language for over-apologizing and then look at the context.

Second, determine the desired "reward." Of all parts in the habit loop, for the bad habit of over-apologizing, I think this is the trickiest part. Why? Because the question is, what are we seeking by over-apologizing? Is it, as suggested by the Child Mind Institute, that we seek to avoid being viewed in a negative light by peers or authority figures? And if so, then how can we possibly seek to achieve this in another way? Or, if we are making a more concrete ask in the professional sphere, perhaps for a more flexible schedule or a raise, then what we are seeking is a yes. And if a yes is what we are seeking, then we definitely should not begin with an "I'm sorry" for no reason because, as my breast imaging colleague Dr. Katia Dodelzon put it, "From a psychological point of view you are priming the one being asked not to grant you what you are asking for. That is the problem." It certainly is. Yet with all of this in mind, perhaps it can be used as a motivation to modify the routine, the third step in the habit loop. (Another motivation might be the desire to keep apologies genuine and real.)

Third, modify the routine (over-apologizing) by recognizing, at the very least, *when* you are going to make an important ask professionally. Then, even if speaking extemporaneously comes naturally to you, consider practicing what you are going to say, watching your language for unindicated apologies, and striving for directness, with supporting evidence to help with confidence. Write it out and consider practicing it in front of a partner or colleague, friend or pet.

Another framework to consider: Aare you more naturally an adder or subtracter? According to Wang Yip, in an October 2019 article, a simple test to make this determination is to ask yourself, "is it easier for you to cut out junk food from your life? Or is it easier to go to the gym? If it is easier for you to cut out junk food from your life, you are a subtracter.... If it is easier for you to go to the gym, you are an adder."[60] If you are a natural subtracter, then Yip recommends directly that you "cut out any habits you deem to be 'bad' or not helping with your life." In the context of this discussion, this would be cut out the habit of over-apologizing, because as previously discussed, this certainly does not help with your professional life. On the other hand, if you are a natural adder, then Yip recommends "Add habits to 'crowd' out bad habits." I see this as similar to Duhigg's suggestion to modify the routine. In the context of this discussion, this could mean replacing apologetic language with related but less sub-servient verbiage such as please or excuse me. In other words, whenever you hear "I'm sorry" coming out of your mouth when it is not really or genuinely needed, then replace it with please or excuse me, for example.

Taking all of this into account, I still wish there was an app that could help me overcome over-apologizing. In other words, my posture has improved by using the UpRight posture device which buzzes on my back (when I remember to wear it) whenever I start slumping. What if a Fitbit or other application could provide some negative reinforcement and buzz us when over-apologizing was detected? This would allow for a quick identification, and, to the extent possible, "a do-over," after a buzz, for example, you could follow with, "let me start again," or "let me rephrase," followed by more robust verbiage.

Need more motivation to overcome over-apologizing? Consider the work of neuroscientist Tara Swart, who says "serial apologists" mostly do so out of habit, perhaps stemming from a childhood where they were made to feel wrong or fearful of punishment. According to Swart, "Apologizing when we have done something wrong is a real strength, but compulsive apologizing presents as a weakness at work and in personal relationships."[61] To eliminate the bad habit of over-apologizing, Swart offers the following three recommendations:

1. Practice self-awareness.

2. Change your vocabulary.

3. Be confident and intentional.

There are limitations to the "stop over-apologizing" pearl. First, many people find it hard to even see and or admit that they have been wrong, let alone apologize; if you fall into this camp, then this might be the first thing to work on. This is because the related *under* apologizing can also be detrimental to relationships, personal and professional. Second, there are definitely cultural differences in the use of "I'm sorry" that should be taken into account, as the first section of this chapter illustrated. Yet if you are like many or most girls and women raised in Western society (and likely beyond) today, you are more likely to fall into the over-apologizing cohort and if so, then this chapter is for you—and for me too.

Conclusion

The purpose of this chapter was to discuss the importance of striving to overcome over-apologizing. Over-apologizing projects weakness both professionally and personally. A logical next step, related to replacing I'm sorry with excuse me or please, is to consider the topic of the next chapter: It doesn't hurt to ask politely.

7

It doesn't hurt
to ask politely

The moment I internalized the lesson of this chapter was on a warm sunny day in late May as I strolled down East 86th street in New York City with my daughter Sophia. I remember walking east on the north side of the block while traffic whizzed west— and that at every single fruit stand on the sidewalk we passed, my daughter calmly asked every "fruit man" if he had lychees.

I do not think that I ever ate a lychee until I was in my early thirties, introduced to the delicacy by a Costa Rican-born friend, Angie, who patiently waited each season for the chewy sweet fruit to hit the fruit stands or certain supermarkets as New York warmed up. Even after Angie moved away, we always remember that just in time for Sophia's birthday at the end of May or around Memorial Day, this small round tropical fruit makes its appearance in the U.S. north east, and so my daughter persisted: Let's ask that fruit man if he has any lychees!

After a handful of stops, my desire to ask waned, but without the goods, Sophia persisted. Finally, mid-block we asked the same

question politely: "Excuse me, Sir, do you have any lychees yet?" And were rewarded with, "Yes, I do, how many pounds would you like?" It doesn't hurt to ask politely.

While "it doesn't hurt to ask politely" sounds like it might be related to something a manners-minded mother might impart to her child, in this case, the teaching was flowing the other way. "Mentorship is bi-directional," my mentor, sponsor, breast imaging colleague and professional friend Dr. Geraldine McGinty has said on several occasions in the professional sphere. It is true in the personal sphere as well, as evidenced by Sophia driving home the lesson to me that it doesn't hurt to ask politely, because if you do, then you may get what you want. If you don't, then there is no way you will.

Overview of the chapter lesson

First, I will provide a focused review of the literature on the topic at hand. Second, I will discuss the psychology related to asking, or not asking. Third, I offer you a case study from my professional sphere on advocating for paid family / medical leave, and what happens when you don't—and do—ask politely.

Focused review of the literature

One of the best articles I have read on the topic of women and asking is from the radiology literature, in the *Journal of the American College of Radiology (JACR)*, by one of only eleven (at the time of this writing) female ACR gold medal winners, Dr. Carol Rumack, who was also the first president of the American Association for Women in Radiology (AAWR). Dr. Rumack wrote the pertinently-titled paper, "Women Don't Ask," articulating that, "There are many social pressures discouraging women from asking. Social expectations typically include that women should wait to be asked to marry, to join a team, or to be promoted. This creates anxiety for women because they prefer not to take a risk and offend their peers. An important concept is that women see control as external or outside themselves…[and] failure as resulting from their personal weaknesses."[62] Note the recurring theme of multiple sources of anxiety for women.

Dr. Rumack then considers what happens if women in medicine do *not* ask, and answers, "Promotions do not occur from hard work alone. Accomplishments that are not visible to a leader or chair of a department will certainly not result in a promotion." In other words, if you do not speak up about your professional achievements, and those with the power to advance and promote you are accordingly unaware, then accomplishments alone will not get you moving up the proverbial professional ladder. On the other hand, continues Dr. Rumack, realistically, "there certainly can be problems arising from strong assertiveness and a very demanding style. A woman may be called too bossy or too emotional, and if she is very shy and submissive, she may be called too nice." [63] Thus, professional women at work may find themselves in a stressful catch-22 situation from where there is no escape because of mutually conflicting circumstances: don't speak up about your achievements and you don't get noticed / promoted; speak up assertively about your achievements and you are negatively viewed. What to do?

In addition to helping others at work with public congratulations of their accomplishments to increase visibility (e.g., sending a division email noting someone's new publication, copying the department chair), what I have done is to add "politely" to the end of my recommendation that "it doesn't hurt to ask." In other words, it *could* hurt to ask in the "wrong" way, where wrong in our society unfortunately continues to mean anything from assertive or demanding, bossy or emotional, to shy or submissive, depending on the circumstances. On the other hand, polite is defined as having a manner or behavior that is considerate and respectful of others. Proceeding in this manner, if women *do* ask, then, "Their view of risk changes from asking for too much and becomes asking for more," says Dr. Rumack. "Positive results are likely to include getting more resources to be successful. They begin their jobs with appropriate salaries and benefits. They start with space and time to advance the organization as well."[64] Starting an ask with politely pointing out a mutually shared goal (e.g., advancement of the institution at which you work) is also an effective opening strategy.

In the non-radiology literature, in *Nice Girls Don't Get the Corner Office* by internationally recognized executive coach Lois P. Frankel, the author describes over 100 behaviors that women learn in childhood that are not helpful to them professionally. Mistake #54 is particularly applicable here: "Failure to negotiate. Don't equate negotiation with confrontation."[65] In other words, Frankel posits that women fail to negotiate because they equate negotiation with confrontation. The corollary of this is that if women reframe negotiation in a way that does not equate it with confrontation, then they are more likely to negotiate and ask for what they want. However, this may be easier said than done, because of very real psychological and physical reasons experienced in the setting of conflict. For example, in a 2020 study in the *Journal of the American Medical Association (JAMA)*, female surgeons experiencing a workplace conflict reported feeling not only self-doubt, but also – yes, again – anxiety and depression. Though not as frequent, this same cohort of female surgeons also reported physical symptoms including gastrointestinal issues, insomnia, and exhaustion.

There very well may be some teleological or evolutionary

reasons for why these experiences hold true. There are also systemic, workplace cultural or cultural in general longstanding inequities and or implicit biases which contribute to this which need to be changed. And yet given that this may take generations, that there is no quick fix, professional women still need a working plan to move forward in the current landscape. This, I have found, is to courageously remember to stand up and ask politely for what is needed and wanted.

That being said, at the same time, I do feel a little sad that I feel like being polite needs to be a part of asking. I hope—and know—that there are many women stronger than me who may not feel this way and hopefully by intentional choices the professional working mothers of today will raise the next generation of professional working mothers where there are fewer social pressures discouraging women from asking. The reason I feel a little sad about including "polite" is because as the saying goes, "Well-behaved women seldom make history," and in this case, well-behaved and polite are somewhat synonymous. On the other hand, I am trying to be gentle with my temperament and limitations; for me, as I suspect is the case for many women, even just the asking feels big and bold. And it may be. Moreover, there may be other times when, better than asking politely, it would be more effective and desirable to state plainly what you would like to do and why – and or just do it. There may be many things, personally and professionally, where just as you should not be over-apologizing, you should not be over-asking. Ask yourself, do I really need to ask permission to do this anyway? Sometimes the answer may be yes, and yet many other times the answer may be no; in the latter, don't ask, just do.

All that being said, please note that "always" and "never" are not included in the "it doesn't hurt to ask politely" phrase because in life there are generally exceptions to rules. But exceptions are exceptions, a special case or inconsistency. Rather this rule or lesson is meant to be a general guiding principle, which more times than not, is one by which to live, in contrast to the status quo of women not asking. For greater personal and professional satisfaction and success, this needs to change. How? Before we tackle this weighty question, the psychology of asking, or not, may be helpful to consider.

Related psychology of asking, or not

The idea of people-pleasing seems somehow related to not asking, or feeling like the only way to ask is politely. Yes, there is absolutely an intrinsic joy to making other people happy, as in "it is better to give than to get." However, beyond that, research has shown that there may be gender differences in this as well. For example, according to a 2017 Pew Research Center study, "empathy, nurturing, and kindness ranked as the second most valued trait in women—but it was number seven for men. So, tend and befriend is no longer just a biological trait. It's an enduring societal pressure: If you want to be liked (or safe from anxieties, real or imagined), you'd better be nice."[66] This pressuring expectation may account, incidentally, for the wild success of the Disney movie *Frozen*. I cried when I saw it on stage in the Broadway musical production in February 2020 with my two older girls right before the COVID-19 pandemic hit. "*Frozen* is one of those wonderfully scripted movies that targets young girls but also resonates with sisters, mothers, and grandmothers alike," wrote the *Huffington Post* in a 2014 article. "Beyond being entertaining, the movie delivers an important message for women of all ages: Stop trying to please everyone, forget perfection, don't be afraid to be different and be true to yourself. Stop being a 'good girl.'"[67]

I saw *Frozen* with my two older daughters as part of a girls' weekend I organized for us in February 2020 to celebrate my promotion to full Professor of Radiology while my husband was away on a work trip. With a lovely dinner with work colleagues planned for March 2020 to celebrate in my professional sphere, it was important to me to celebrate with my daughters as well because they have been with me along the path from resident trainee to full Professor.

I was 30 years old when my first daughter, Sophia, was born (2008) at the end of my third year of diagnostic radiology residency, and the experience I went through to carve out sufficient maternity leave ignited my passion for advocating for improved family and medical leave policies—and all of this relates to it doesn't hurt to ask politely. One of the many reasons women need to get promoted is that real titles *do* matter because they give you gravitas and can make you more effective in advocating for positive change. I was 33 years old when my second daughter, Michaela, was born—intentionally one year and two days after I became an Assistant Professor of Radiology so I could get the full twelve weeks of leave under the 1993 Family Medical Leave Act (FMLA). This was not an option when I was a resident, before the Supreme Court ruled in 2011 in Mayo Foundation v. US that medical residents have employee status (thus FMLA-eligible). I was 39 years old when my third daughter, Giordana, was born and maternity leave then, I saw, was the easiest professionally to take because I had some clout by title and promotion to Associate Professor of Radiology. So, while I have always been clear that my children are my priority in my life, along the way, my children have seen me work long hours, travel to conferences to give talks—often accompanying me—and seen first-hand from the inside some of what it takes to be a successful woman professionally. Thus, it was important to me for them to see that it is worth celebrating when a huge life goal is achieved. It is also important to celebrate small victories along the way.

Sheryl Sandberg has also spoken to the point of the importance of women in power to help create more family friendly workplace policies. For example, in her 2013 best-selling book *Lean In: Women, Work and the Will to Lead*, Sandberg writes about pregnancy parking: "To this day, I'm embarrassed that I didn't realize that pregnant women needed reserved parking until I experienced my own aching feet....other pregnant women must have suffered in silence, not wanting to ask for special treatment. Or maybe they lacked the confidence or seniority to demand that the problem be fixed. Having one pregnant woman at the top... made the difference."[68] However, you don't have to—and shouldn't have to—wait to get to the top, to make a difference in your life (and potentially others) by asking for what you need or want. Why suffer in silence when you can ask politely? Because asking can feel burdensomely hard to do. Sometimes a step-by-step approach can be helpful.

(In)Sufficient paid parental leave: What happens when you don't—and do—ask politely: A Case Study

I have been passionate about improving family/medical leave in radiology since 2007/8 when I was pregnant with my first child as a third-year radiology resident. While I didn't suffer in silence to get the maternity leave I needed, I stressed and agonized every time I had to ask along the way. Imagining that my experience was similar to many others, and that many would choose to suffer in silence rather than ask, I eventually decided to start asking politely on a larger scale, taking a step-by-step approach inspired by a hero of mine, former U.S. Supreme Court Justice Ruth Bader Ginsberg. But first, a bit about my initial experience which inspired it all.

Like many professional arenas, the world of physicians is very hierarchical. At the bottom of the rung are medical students: first, second, third and fourth years. After graduating from medical school and receiving their medical doctor (MD) degree, newly minted doctors are still in training or "trainees" during their residency, in which they are learning their chosen area of specialty; these are the post-graduate years (PGY), PGY-1 (internship), PGY-2, PGY-3 and so on. After completing residency and taking the appropriate board-certifying exams, at academic institutions, one is known as an attending physician and may begin to supervise residents in training, as well as climb the academic ranks from instructor in their specialty to assistant professor, associate professor, and full professor.

I was pregnant with my first baby (the one who years later would persistently go after the lychees) when I was a PGY-4 resident in radiology and thus had little to no autonomy over my schedule. This was controlled by the chief residents; elected by co-residents and faculty, they are well respected senior residents whose administrative responsibilities including making the schedule for all years of residents. The first iteration of my upcoming maternity leave I was presented with by "the chiefs" (two men at the time) was four weeks, that is, my annually allotted vacation and a standard block of time on the schedule. The chiefs were well meaning, just trying to balance the schedule and yet like their peers across the country were equipped without a bit of training on parental leave policies. Understandably, without any clear accessible guidelines, they went with male common sense: vacation, the four allotted weeks. And yet I was, for the first time, even before my child was born, presented with the wrenching pull between my child and my profession. I was so shocked and horrified that I might only get twenty days off from work to bond with my infant that my passion for advocating for sufficient parental leave was born, before my baby. With my horror, came clarity: If I don't ask politely for more time off, and provide the rationale for why I should get it, then my priority in life—my child(ren)—will be negatively impacted.

And so began my family leave research. I started at the institutional level and GME (graduate medical education) policies; I looked into what my medical specialty, diagnostic radiology, had to say at the national level; I read about federal policy with the 1993 Family and Medical Leave Act (FMLA) signed into effect by former President Bill Clinton; and gape-mouthed, I read internationally to learn about the (much higher) standard of care for maternity leave in other countries. I learned a great deal that then that would serve as a basis for work I continue to do now to strive for improved paid family/medical leave in our specialty; I also learned, or rather it became clear to me in the process of the research, that I would have to bide my time until I had traveled sufficiently up the ranks of the medical hierarchy in order to really make a difference for others. In other words, I realized that there was only so much I could do as a resident to advocate for myself and my unborn baby individually at this point. I would need to stand by for the moment. And yet it was the time when I set a huge goal for my entire professional career: improve family/ medical leave in my professional environment. It seemed (and seems) deeply hypocritical that the profession which was telling people how and why to best take care of themselves was not doing the same internally. If the medical professional was supposed to be or behave with the highest integrity, and integrity for me includes meaning practicing what you preach, then the medical profession was failing in integrity with respect to family / medical leave.

But circling back to the practical things I learned then in 2008, a few months before my first baby was born in May. Email exchanges at the time between me and "the chiefs" cited law and precedents related to maternity and family medical leave, including:

1. Federal Government Family and Medical Leave Act (FMLA)

Synopsis of Law: Covered employers must grant an eligible employee up to a total of 12 workweeks of unpaid leave during any 12-month period for one or more of the following reasons:

- for the birth and care of the newborn child of the employee.

- for placement with the employee of a son or daughter for adoption or foster care.

- to care for an immediate family member (spouse, child, or parent) with a serious health condition; or

- to take medical leave when the employee is unable to work because of a serious health condition. http://www.dol.gov/esa/whd/fmla/

2. American Board of Radiology: Leave of Absence Policy

Leave of absence: *Leaves of absence and vacation may be granted to residents at the discretion of the program director in accordance with local rules. Within the required period(s) of* *graduate medical education, the total such leave and vacation time may not exceed SIX CALENDAR WEEKS (30 working days) for residents in a program for one year, TWELVE CALENDAR WEEKS (60 working days) for residents in a program for two years, EIGHTEEN CALENDAR WEEKS (90 working days) for residents in a program for three years, or TWENTY FOUR CALENDAR WEEKS (120 working days) for residents in a program for four years. If a longer leave of absence is granted, the required period of graduate medical education must be extended accordingly.* http://www.theabr.org/DR_Pri_Req.htm

3. Cornell GME: Leave of Absence Policy

A Leave of absence is an excused absence from work for an approved reason. A leave of absence can be used for a maximum of no more than 26 weeks an academic calendar year (7/1 – 6/30).

Employees may request leaves of absence for one of three reasons:

1. personal illness

2. to care for a family member who is ill; or

3. other valid personal reasons.

In sum, at an institutional, specialty and federal level, I was entitled to at least twelve weeks of (unpaid) maternity leave and so putting my inner, people-pleasing "good girl" aside, I asked politely for twelve weeks of leave, presenting the above objective information and policies to the chair of my department and the department's legal and compliance officer. My request was granted. I do not know what went on behind the scenes. Most importantly, my chair, among other things, is a kind and fair leader, and had been a mentor and sponsor of mine for five years already. Yet, I can imagine that behind closed doors, the discussion with legal and compliance was about what federal law mandated as opposed to what the organization may have wanted to do. I learned a great deal, including the nascent growing understanding inside that it doesn't hurt to ask politely. If I had not asked, then there was *no* possibility I would have secured twelve weeks of maternity leave as a resident, maybe one of the first ever for a medical resident in the United States. I have no way of definitely knowing, however research by Dr. Kirti Magudia et al published over ten years later supports this hypothesis with a study describing "childbearing and family leave at 15 graduate medical education (GME)–sponsoring institutions affiliated with 12 US medical schools on top 10 lists for funding or ranking," and finding that "The mean duration of maternity leave (encompassing both childbirth leave and designated family leave available to childbearing mothers) was 6.6 weeks (range, 2-10 weeks)."[69]

Fast forward to 2015: I was no longer at the near-bottom of the medical pecking order, no longer the most junior rank. I had worked hard and was by then an Associate Professor of Radiology at the institution where I had trained and nationally, on the Board of Directors of the American Association for Women in Radiology (AAWR) in an automatic succession leading to President in 2019. I gratefully joined this path at the AAWR, seeing it as an opportunity to use power for positive change, since part of the AAWR's mission is to identify and address issues faced by women in our specialty. I began by writing a normative piece, informed by my standing in the AAWR, and as a member of both the American College of Radiology (ACR) Commission for Women and Diversity and the ACR Human Resources

Commission. In this capacity, in which I was on both commissions and acted as a liaison between the two, I first-authored an opinion piece with members of both commissions and the legal counsel of the ACR, entitled "The Family and Medical Leave Act Should Be Applicable to All Radiologists and Radiation Oncologists." The most important sentence of this article reads: "Therefore, the ACR Commission for Women and General Diversity and the ACR Commission on Human Resources believe that, when feasible, academic radiology and radiation oncology departments, as well as private practice radiology and radiation oncology groups, should consider providing the aforementioned family leave benefits to all of their eligible female and male employees, including residents, whether or not they are required to do so by federal law (in the case of smaller groups with fewer than 50 employees)." [70]

In 2016, the following year, I began to gather evidence to make my argument or case. The next related article on the topic was a data-driven one entitled "Utilization of the Family and Medical Leave Act in Radiology Practices According to the 2016 ACR Commission on Human Resources Workforce Survey." The purpose of this study "was to assess utilization of FMLA in radiology practices. The principal findings were that most radiologists took FMLA leave to care for a newborn or adopted child (49%), followed by personal serious health condition (42%), to care for an immediate family member (8%), or active military duty (1%). Female radiologists took a greater number of weeks of FMLA leave than male radiologists for all reasons except for military duty. At least 69% of leave time was paid, irrespective of reason for leave or gender of person taking it, but the vast majority of practices (82%) made no workforce changes to cover leaves of absence. With these findings, it becomes evident that, contrary to popular belief, FMLA leave is not just a women's issue, because both genders needed absences from work for FMLA-sanctioned reasons."[71]

In 2017, interested in changing trends in utilization of FMLA in radiology practices—or lack thereof—I submitted a follow-up manuscript on the topic to *JACR*, where both of the aforementioned pieces had previously been published and received *the* rudest rejection letter of my entire career (for example, I "could not understand why you undertook to write the manuscript."), one which left me trying to get a grip by staring at the sticky note on my office wall on which I had printed, "Take criticism seriously, but not personally" – Hillary Clinton. Politics aside, I now share this rejection letter as a teaching point when lecturing to other radiologists about publishing in radiology to drive home the importance of this quotation and persistence.

Postscript: I kept asking politely and this article was subsequently published in a competitor journal in 2018. Postscript #2: When I became an Editor-in-Chief in my own right, the first female editor-in-chief of a radiology journal,[72] I personally reviewed each and every one of the template letters that go to authors and revised them to convey respect, understanding and kindness. For example, the journal's rejection letter status post review now reads, "The reviewer comments support the final decision of reject; however, I hope that the suggestions below may be helpful to you in revising the manuscript and hopefully achieving successful publication in another journal. Respectfully, Elizabeth Kagan Arleo MD, Editor-in-Chief."

By 2019, I was President of the AAWR, and authored an opinion piece for *JACR* entitled "Paid Parental Leave in Radiology: The Time Is Now-Challenges, Strategies, and the Business Case for Implementation," opening that "The time for sufficient paid parental leave in radiology—12 weeks—is now. Compared with the rest of the world, the United States is far behind in providing paid leave for working parents with new children...[in 2017] the only country to offer no national statutory entitlement to paid maternity leave. Within the United States, compared with other industries, medicine is far behind in providing paid leave for working parents with new children." The article then went on to cover several reasons radiology leaders should support twelve weeks of paid parental leave, including the compelling reason that it could be good for business, before pointing out that if the Society of Chairs of Academic Radiology Departments (SCARD) were to endorse a statement of support for 12 weeks of paid parental leave, then strategically such an endorsement would provide something for departments to aspire to and for chairs to advocate for at an individual institutional level. (An indirect yet polite ask).

From there, I continued to ask politely by drafting a statement of support for SCARD, which was championed through by SCARD President-Elect Dr. Cheri Canon—the same Dr. Cheri Canon from whom the lesson of the pre-meeting meeting comes. I still remember where I was standing when I learned from Cheri that SCARD had voted to support the statement, subsequently publishing in *JACR* their support for the AAWR and pledge to strive for change that provides 12 weeks of paid parental leave for eligible (as defined by FMLA) faculty members of all genders.

Back to the "Paid Parental Leave in Radiology: The Time Is Now" article. I lost significant sleep over one particular sentence I wrote that addressed the paternalistic nature of board policies as well as the fact they reflected benevolent sexism in action (at the time, if women took 12 weeks of FMLA leave in the first three years of training, then they could not sit for board-certifying exams or graduate on time.) True though it was, because it was *not* polite—they were fighting words—I worried I was going to get a call or email from the American Board of Radiology revoking my board-certification to practice radiology. No correspondence, summons or subpoena arrived, although I suffered in silence imagining other worst-case scenarios.

I will never know what went on behind the scenes, but bottom line is that in the same issue in which SCARD supported the AAWR call for twelve weeks of paid parental leave, the ABR also published in the *JACR* a policy change, allowing up to a 4-month leave of absence (in addition to standard vacation). Note to self: Sometimes when you ask, to get things done, it cannot be polite.

[2022 postscript: In April 2022, nearly a decade and a half after my passion for improving family/medical leave in radiology was ignited, the American College of Radiology (ACR) passed the historic paid family/medical leave (PFML) resolution I was the lead author for at its annual meeting, resolving that "diagnostic radiology, interventional radiology, radiation oncology, medical physics, and nuclear medicine practices, departments and training programs strive to provide 12 weeks of paid family/medical leave in a 12-month period for its attending physicians, medical physicists, and members in training as needed." Next stop? Taking this policy to American Medical Association (AMA) so that it can be extended to other and all medical specialties.

This was done by Dr. Meredith Englander and the ACR, and in November 2022, I received word from Dr. Englander that the AMA adopted policy — with language directly from our aforementioned radiology resolution — to support paid parental leave, specifically recommending that "medical practices, departments, departments and training programs strive to provide 12 weeks of paid parental, family and medical necessity leave in a 12-month period for their attending and trainee physicians as needed."[73]]

Conclusion

The purpose of this chapter was to discuss the important lesson that it doesn't hurt to ask politely. This pearl, too, is not without its limitations, namely, that there are certainly many things for which asking politely is too tepid such as equal pay and opportunities and a harassment free workplace, to name just two. These must be demanded and ensured. However, on a smaller yet still meaningful scale, "it doesn't hurt to ask politely" holds true as a general rule in that if you do not ask politely, then you have little to no chance of getting what you want, personally or professionally. If you do, the worst you can hear is no—and yet you might hear yes. The logical next step, given that I still find it challenging to internalize and live consistently by this rule (and maybe you do too), is to consider the lesson of the next chapter: have a growth mindset.

8

Have a growth mindset

I discovered the principle of the growth mindset when first reading Carol Dweck's seminal 2007 book, *Mindset: The New Psychology of Success.* A growth mindset, as defined by Dweck, is an individual's perception that their abilities can be developed through hard work and commitment to learning. This is in contradistinction to a fixed mindset, in which a person believes that their basic qualities are fixed.

Although Dweck's concept of a growth mindset came way after my personal primary and secondary schooling, I am grateful that this is a concept now being taught in many schools, including my girls'. It is a specific part of their curriculum starting in third grade, complete with a summarizing printable to hang at home desks, which I confess to have copied for myself as well. The concept is a fundamental one, which if genuinely embraced, can lead to success with other lessons in this book and beyond. Why? Because it says, in a nutshell, that our most basic capabilities can progress and be advanced through dedication and diligent effort. If you have read this far in this book, then I suspect you are someone

for whom both values are important as well. If this is the case, and if you too have passed your primary school years and need to learn about growth mindset for yourself as I did, then read on.

Overview of chapter lesson

First, I will present a focused review of the growth mindset literature. Second, I will discuss of how I didn't heed the call of a growth mindset and what it cost me. Third, I consider the related concept of the importance of an atmosphere of growth. Finally, I offer specific ways to develop a growth mindset.

Focused review of the literature

Using the PubMed medical literature search engine, I found sixteen systematic reviews on the topic of growth mindset, including a 2014 study in *Biological Psychology* in which the authors studied the neurocognitive mechanisms behind "mindset" messages that can affect brain activity and function. In the study, participants were randomly assigned to read a passage about intelligence — that it was either flexible and could be developed (growth-mindset), or not (fixed-mindset) – before completing a reaction-time task while an electroencephalogram (EEG, a recording of the electrical activity of the brain) was recorded (methods). The results? Participants who read growth-mindset information had increased attention to task-relevant stimuli, whereas participants who read fixed-mindset information had increased attention to responses, suggesting that "growth- and fixed-mindset messages have differential effects on the neural dynamics underlying cognitive control."[74] In other words, having a growth mindset can affect how your brain works.

Also using the PubMed medical literature search engine, I found sixteen clinical trials on the topic of growth mindset, and one of the most interesting was a 2017 study in the *Journal of Youth and Adolescence* in which authors investigated what a six-week classroom intervention targeting growth mindset yielded about students' daily quality of experience in science classes. Seventh graders were randomly assigned to either a mindset intervention condition or an alternative. Students who were not exposed to the mindset intervention showed a drop in interest, learning, and how much control they felt they had. The opposite was true for the mindset intervention students, suggesting strongly that the brain is both changing and changeable.

How might the studies documenting the benefits of a growth mindset with students be applicable to working professional mothers? Let's start to answer the question by looking at the negative: If you don't heed the call of the growth mindset, then what might it cost you, personally and professionally?

How I didn't always heed the call of the growth mindset, and what that cost (or almost cost) me

There are so many examples of how I didn't heed the call of the growth mindset, because for the first approximately thirty-eight years of my life—until I learned about growth mindset when Sophia was in third grade —I was, I guess by default, a fixed mindset person. I am not proud of it or happy about it, and I am not entirely sure why this was the case, but the reasons are likely multifactorial—part nature, part nurture. Something also makes me feel like there is some connection between having a fixed mindset and being a people-pleaser and over-apologizing unnecessarily. Let me see if I can lay this connection bare. But first: personal examples of fixed mindset.

Example 1, from high school:
"I choke during tennis"

I was the only high school freshman to make the girls varsity tennis team at my high school in the fall of 1991, and yet instead of enjoying my victory, the pressure at age fourteen to win led to me to "choke" on the court. According to *Sports Psychology for Tennis*, choking – in tennis - is when a motivated player experiences decreased performance as a result of fear of failure. The "choking" analogy is apt, because choking medically is when oxygen is cut off from the brain due to an object physically obstructing an airway; similarly, choking in tennis is when a driven player is cut off from success to anxiety mentally obstructing performance. This is exactly what I experienced: the mental stress of competing and potentially failing was so unpleasant I thought I could not get past it, that it was fixed, and the next year I chose to pursue the yearbook as an after-school activity instead. What this cost me – notwithstanding that I immensely enjoyed the yearbook — is the joy that playing tennis originally brought to me and many important life lessons. I now see that tennis is an amazing analogy for life as well: Play one point at a time, and then move on. Focus on the present, not the past point that happened or the future points to come, but the point being played in the moment so you can do your best.

Example 2, from medical school:
"I'm bad at physics"

I went to medical school to become an Ob/Gyn given my long-standing interest in women's health dating back to my middle or high school biology classes with beloved science teacher, Barbara Silber. However, by mid third year of medical school, realizing that I never wanted to be in the operating room ever again, I confronted the reality of needing to choose a different specialty.

Research with an incredible interventional radiologist and mentor, Dr. Michael Tal, showed me I could pursue my interest in women's health through diagnostic radiology. The problem? To become a board-certified radiologist at the time required sitting for dedicated physics boards and despite working my bottom off in high school and college, I could never obtain a grade better than a B in physics. "I'm not good at physics" almost stopped me from going into radiology. Fortunately, the desire to pursue what I was interested in trumped this fear, and I decided I would deal with the physics boards when the time came. I did. And yet my fixed mindset that "I'm not good at physics" almost cost me my medical specialty.

Example 3, from my thirties and forties regarding cooking: "I can't cook."

Home economics is something I missed en route to becoming a doctor and I have congenital anosmia (born without a sense of smell for no apparent reason; in contrast to acquired anosmia, for example, secondary to a COVID-19 infection) so cooking was not something I had done much of because "I can't cook." What this fixed mindset cost me was among other things, money spent on take out or going out that I could have saved if I knew how to cook myself. The pandemic changed many things, including how I thought about the kitchen. Inspired by the book and film *Julie and Julia*, in which a food blogger named Julie Powell cooks all the recipes in Julia Child's first cook book in a year, I decided to cook my way through the 185 recipes in *How to Cook Everything: The Basics* by Mark Bittman, an American food journalist, author, and former columnist for *The New York Times*. I really like to eat (part of why I exercise regularly is to eat) and to go out to restaurants when possible, so cooking all these recipes helped me not to miss things during extended self-imposed quarantine in the beginning of the COVID-19 pandemic. In fact, I ended up eating more of a variety of foods then I ever had when we went to restaurants. Most importantly, I learned that I could learn how to cook, no sense of smell and all. Adopting a growth mindset allowed me to shift from "I can't cook" to "I can't cook yet . . . and I can learn how if it is a priority."

As the above examples from my life illustrate, what happens when you don't apply and adopt the principle of a growth mindset is that you live with a fixed mindset and thus limit your options. Too many options are not necessarily a good thing, because too many options can be overwhelming and can lead to decision fatigue and the impossible pursuit of perfectionism, as previously discussed. But options that you may want to pursue but do not because of a fixed mindset? That is not a good outcome, because you are not living up to your true potential. You may hold yourself back from doing things that would bring you joy if you did them, holding yourself back because of fear of failure. How to overcome this?

What I had to overcome to take the first step
Overcoming a fixed mindset lens of looking at the world is not easy. For me, what has helped, is when doing my weekly, monthly, quarterly, and annual planning, professionally and personally, using the tripartite framework of Self, Relationships and Career (courtesy of Laura Vanderkam), with further refinement of the first category to include the subcategories of Mind, Body and Spirit (or Intellectual, Physical and Emotional). Specifically, though, related to the focus of this chapter, I want to circle in on the first of these three elements—mind—which for me, in this planning context, means an environment of a growth mindset.

This is supported by writings by Gretchen Rubin, who puts forth that for happiness, "you also need to feel growth—a sense of learning, of betterment, of advancement, of contributing to the growth of others."[75] This, in a sense, is the essence of a growth mindset.

So, with the growth mindset I am learning to cook. I drive even though I am sometimes fearful of it, having been born and raised in NYC where having a car can be more of a pain than a necessity. I am writing this book. At the moment I write this sentence, I am not done with any of these three; they and I are a work in progress and the growth mindset supports this. Writes Carol Dweck in *Mindset*, "This growth mindset is based on the belief that your basic qualities are things you can cultivate through your efforts. Although people may differ in every which way in their initial talents and aptitudes, interests or temperaments, everyone can change and grow through application and experience."[76] All that being said, here are my top 10 tips for developing a growth mindset, inspired by Saga Briggs, managing editor for InformED:[77]

1. "Yet" – use the word (as in, I don't know how to cook…yet).
2. Take criticism seriously, not personally.
3. Lessons learned - reflect on your day or week (or beyond) by writing them down.
4. Mistakes – learn from yours and others.
5. Imperfections – embrace and accept them.
6. Grit – try to develop it.
7. Re-frame challenges as opportunities for self-improvement.
8. Experiment with different learning strategies.

9. Prioritize learning over (seeking) approval.
10. Value process over product.

Of all of the above, #1 about using the word yet is my favorite, because I find it extremely effective in effectively flipping a switch from a fixed- to a growth- mindset with just one little three letter word. I've engaged my daughters to make it a group effort in that, if any of us hear another saying, "I can't X," then one of us (ideally) replies.... yet.

The major limitation I find in the pearl "have a growth mindset" is that there are *so* many ways I still want to grow and develop as a mother, wife, daughter, doctor, friend, athlete, and writer—and yet time is limited and finite. For this, I think about seasons of my life. For example, my children are no longer babies so I have I little more bandwidth for avocational pursuits like writing this book; and yet they are still young and living at home and this too will pass. I enjoyed learning to cook during the initial months of the COVID-19 pandemic; and yet there will be more time for me to develop as a home chef when that is no longer the case.

Conclusion

The purpose of this chapter was to discuss the growth mindset. The principal finding is that understanding and ideally genuinely internalizing that ones' abilities are not fixed but rather can be developed can have a profound effect on ones' personal and professional development and ultimately happiness in life, as hopefully all the lessons in this book can as well. The logical next step is to think about how you can take the lessons from this book into the real world of your life, if you are interested and choose to do so.

Conclusion:

How to take these pearls into the world

Review of what you have learned

The purpose of this book is to share with you, my fellow professional working mothers, some of the pearls that have helped me stay sane, productive, and growing. This book is in no way an exhaustive list of every possible lesson, nor is it a list that just because it works for me will necessarily work for you. Rather, it is my hope that in sharing a more personal side of my story, there will be something in here that resonates with you, inspires you, or helps you in some way to manage the challenges of a professional career and the challenges of parenthood, either one a challenge in its own respect, together a double whammy.

In summary, the eight pearls or lessons learned are as follows:

1. Eat your frog

2. 168 hours: you actually have more time that you think

3. If you fail to plan, you are planning to fail

4. Remember the pre-meeting meeting…and that you are not an impostor

5. Don't let the perfect be the enemy of the good

6. Stop over-apologizing

7. It doesn't hurt to ask politely

8. Have a growth mindset

Pearl one is the titular missive to eat your frog, meaning that if something is important, then try to do it towards the beginning of or as early as possible in the day, week, month, quarter, or year. Doing so can set you up for success and lessen your mental load. I challenge you to become a "frog eater par-excellence!" Putting your frog on the calendar can be a great first step. And remember, per Mark Twain, it it's your job to eat two frogs, then start with the bigger one.

Pearl two is to keep in mind that you actually have more time than you think: 168 hours every week. Mathematically, this means that even if you work 50 hours (more than many) and sleep 56 hours (8 hours a night x 7 days a week) each week, then 50 + 56 = 106 hours, which means you still have 62 hours after work and sleep for yourself (including your mind, body and spirit; or intellectual, physical and emotional pursuits) and your relationships (including your children, partner, other family, and friends). This further means that it is not accurate to say you do not have time for something; rather "I don't have time" means—given the above math—it is not a priority, which is okay; we all have different priorities. Think about what your priority is for a given time period and schedule it in—with accountability if needed—because it is largely your choice how to spend your time.

Pearl three—if you fail to plan, you are planning to fail—is thus related. The corollary of this, with a positive reframe, is that planning sets you up for success. Planning successfully means having a methodology like Getting Things Done (GTD) and associated tools that you can use to help you achieve your priority(s) in your personal and professional spheres of responsibility, such as a paper planner like the Full Focus Planner if you still enjoy one and a productivity app such as ToDoIst. Planning successfully also means planning regularly (daily, weekly, monthly, quarterly) with generous time estimates, buffers, and flexibility, all of which will further help set yourself up for success and sanity.

Pearl four is to remember the pre-meeting meeting and that you are not an impostor; the goal is to adopt the former (the pre-meeting meeting) and abandon the latter (Impostor Syndrome). In other words, keep in mind that at meetings, key decisions have often already been made prior to the start of the gathering; men have pre-meetings in which they may discuss how they will vote and key talking points, and women should do the same. To be confident at meetings, pre- or otherwise, also remember that you are *not* an impostor; to combat Impostor Syndrome use the 5Rs (Recognize it; Rational thinking; Reframe; Ready; Repeat if recurrent).

Pearl five is pertinent whether we're talking about the aforementioned meeting(s) or just getting dinner on the table: don't let the perfect be the enemy of the good. This can mean, as Sheryl Sandberg put it even more succinctly, that done is better than perfect. This does *not* mean making rubbish—rather it means that instead of striving for perfection, choose to be a satisficer; set criteria, and when criteria are met, then this signals completion. Perfect takes too long and there is an opportunity cost or tradeoff to everything. Again as Laura Vanderkam wrote, "Expectations are infinite. Time is finite. You are always choosing. Choose well."[78]

Pearl six is to stop-over apologizing. This means stop apologizing too often or when there is no actual reason to do so. "Apologizing when we have done something wrong is a real strength," writes Tara Swart, "but compulsive apologizing presents as a weakness at work and in personal relationships,"[79] providing the rationale for why we should stop. How to do so? Listening to your verbiage and changing your vocabulary if needed (for example, replacing "I'm sorry" with "please" or "excuse me") is a good start.

Pearl seven is that it doesn't hurt to ask politely. Doing so politely means your request is respectful and considerate of others while at the same time advocating for yourself and others. What is the worst that could happen? That you might hear no... but you could hear yes, and if you do not even ask in the first place, then there is no way a response in the affirmative can come about. Proceeding in this manner, if women *do* ask, then, "Their view of risk changes from asking for too much," writes ACR gold medal winner Dr. Carol Rumack, "and becomes asking for more."[80]

Pearl eight, have a growth mindset, is important in and of itself, as well as to support all the previous pearls. A growth mindset means that "people believe that their most basic abilities can be developed through dedication and hard work—brains and talent are just the starting point. This view creates a love of learning and a resilience that is essential for great accomplishment."[81] One of the most effective ways to develop a growth mindset yourself and in your relationships is simply with one three-letter word: yet. Hear yourself saying, out loud or in your head, "I can't plan" or "I'm not good at planning"? Then tack on "yet" at the end of each so that your verbiage reflects the more positive mental attitude of "I'm not good at planning...yet."

How to take these lessons into the world

Thank you very much, Elizabeth, and yet how do I take these lessons into the world, you may ask? Good question. To use a radiology report (my more common form of writing) analogy, the book up until this point features my findings and impressions, some of the key lessons I have learned as a professional working mother so far. What is needed now are recommendations or a management plan. If any of these lessons resonate with you and you are interested in trying to adopt them as your own, then I would recommend the following.

First, for any lessons or pearls that resonated with you, write them out by hand and place them where you will see them regularly, such as your office or planner. Why write by hand? Why a place where you will see them regularly? Rationale: handwritten notetaking is beneficial for two reasons, according to Princeton and UCLA researchers in a 2016 study published in *Psychological Science*. The first reason has to do with the encoding hypothesis, referring to the mental processing that occurs to improve learning and retention when a person is taking notes by hand. The second reason has to do the external-storage hypothesis, which posits that you learn by being able to look back at your notes, or even the notes of other people. Finally, posting the lessons where you will see them may be enough to follow through for some, where others may need more external accountability in some way.

Second, for any and all pearls that do not resonate with you, do *not* write them onto the aforementioned hand-written list; instead leave blank lines to fill in your own personal lessons or pearls as they come to you. A part of using my paper planner is my workday shutdown ritual, which not only includes reviewing my calendar and ToDoIst for the day closing and the next two days, but also trying to write down two lessons learned, even if they are small or quotidian (for example, a recent one I wrote down, courtesy of my friend Samantha, is the bathroom trick. Here's the lesson: When you're at a restaurant and a child is saying, "When is the food coming, when is the food coming?!" a walk to the bathroom may provide a practical distraction and result in food on the table when you return. In my planner, for conciseness, I would just write, under Lessons Learned: Samantha's restaurant bathroom trick.) For happiness, an atmosphere of growth can be important, as discussed in the previous chapter, thus reflecting and writing daily lessons learned may lead over time to larger lessons learned or emergence of personal pearls.

Third, and finally, these lessons or pearls, unlike the ten commandments supposedly, are *not* written in stone: revisit and revise, remove and or replace. They may evolve as you learn more about yourself, and as your relationships and career grow and evolve as well.

Practical next steps for the reader now that the book is over

If you have come this far, then I have several practical next steps for you the reader now that the book is over.

First, as described above, write out the lessons or pearls that resonate with you; leave blank lines for future lessons; revisit and revise, remove and or replace the ones written down; and then actually place them where you will see them regularly; get an accountability partner if needed.

Second, read or listen to *Getting Things Done* by David Allen.[82] If you work outside the home, depending on the length of your commute and how many days per week you do it, you can through the book pretty quickly by pairing the tasks of commuting and listening. This strategy can work well when you're seeking to form a new habit that isn't fully established yet, because you're pairing it with something you won't forget to do, like commute. If you work from home, then consider pairing listening to GTD with something mindless that also has to get done, like emptying the dishwasher or putting away the laundry.

Third, if you have any electronic devices—and if you are a professional working mother, then chances are that you probably have several—then download the free version of the app ToDoIst. This takes no more than one minute. Then in the Project section, start by making several context-based (ala GTD) projects to get yourself started, for example, Home, Office, Errands, Calls, Email. Then, every time you enter a task in one of these respective projects (or projects to come), follow it with parentheses including a number, where the number represents your time estimate for how long you think it will take to complete the task. Then to build buffers, consider adding up to 50 percent more to this time estimate. Add a date to start doing the task and you are already making good progress towards getting things done.

If you do these above three practical steps alone, then you will be well on your way in terms of taking the lessons of this book into world, in wearing and owning these pearls, so to speak. If you would like to do more, and you still like using paper and pens in your planning, then I also highly recommend the Full Focus Planner, which can be used for daily, weekly and quarterly planning and beyond.

What to expect now that the reader has pearls for transformation

Now that you have my pearls for transformation, I hope that they will help you as a professional working mother to lead *not* a perfect life—don't let perfect be the enemy of the good—but rather a satisfying personal and professional life in which you are happy and content, at ease and in peace and less overwhelmed. Although I am definitely more in touch with my intellectual side than my spiritual, the latter two phrases—adapted from *Mindful Birthing: Training the Mind, Body, and Heart for Childbirth and Beyond* by nurse midwife Nancy Bardacke[83]—are part of something I sometimes say to myself in the evening in bed after I have turned out the lights, thinking of my family slumbering nearby or wherever they may be:

May we be safe and protected

May we be healthy in body and in mind

May we be happy and content

May we live with ease and in peace, in an atmosphere of growth* *(* not in Bardacke's original text, something I have added on)*

Tiffany Dufu, in her 2017 notable book, *Drop the Ball: Achieving More by Doing Less,*[84] talks about developing manifestos. Maybe my one for my family above will inspire you to think about one for you and yours, or for your work life, or for your life overall. This is another way of thinking about the 50,000-foot view in Allen's *Getting Things Done*, considering your life's purpose. These are all of course deeply personal. As this book comes to a close, I will share my professional manifesto for my work, which is to be, with integrity and kindness, an accurate and compassionate physician and to give back to my profession through mentorship and sponsorship.

Hope and vision for the reader

In closing, my hope and vision for the reader, based on where I am in my life today: may we find enjoyable and meaningful the process of striving to cultivate both a satisfying personal and professional life, not only for ourselves but also as role models for our children and potentially the next generation of professional working mothers to come.

In bocca al lupo!*

(Italian, colloquial, essentially meaning good luck, literally translated "into the wolf's mouth." Like the English theatrical slang "break a leg," the Italian phrase "in bocca al lupo" compares any challenging situation to being caught in the sharp jaws of a wild canine. The appropriate response, in Italian? "Crepi lupo!" meaning "kill the wolf!")*

Acknowledgments

I acknowledge with gratitude, roughly in chronological order of appearance in my life:

My mother, Lillian S. Kagan PhD, my first role model of a successful professional working mother; and my father, Joseph Edward Arleo PhD, author of two novels—it is because of you that I too have had this huge life goal to publish a book. Words are insufficient to thank both of you for the love and life you have given me.

My half siblings, Ted, Adrian (another professional working mother) and Michael Arleo; I am grateful for you all and seek more ways to share life together.

Professional mentors and sponsors who have positively impacted my career in tremendous ways, including (but not limited to) Harvey Kliman MD PhD, Michael Tal MD MBA,, Howard Forman MD MBA, Robert J. Min MD MBA, Geraldine McGinty MD MBA, Hedvig Hricak MD PhD, Kasia Macura MD PhD, Carol

Rumack MD, Cheri Canon MD, Etta Pisano MD, and Stephanie Spottswood MD MSPH—I strive to pay it forward through my own mentorship and sponsorship of the next generation, with you all as role models.

My husband, Joshua W. Thompson, who by action and words, has truly demonstrated to me and our daughters that my work is just as important as his; supported me every step of the way professionally since we met when I was in medical school, without complaint about time given to my profession; and, as life partner, made my dreams come true with the creation together of our three extraordinary daughters.

Dear caregivers throughout the years who have enabled me to be a professional working mother by covering our children so I could cover patient care, including Wynne Cruz, Angie Brooks Rice, Joanne McHenry, and Daria Radmilo—I couldn't have done what I've done and continue to do without you, and you all hold a special place in my heart.

My literary agent, Peter Garlid, who believed in *Frog* and found publisher Armin Lear Press and editor Maryann Karinch—thank you both so very much for believing in me, making my work better, and helping me to achieve this huge life goal. Also, thanks to my first official reader, Gretel Hakanson of KN Literary Arts and to Kelly Notaras herself for her inspirational book, *The Book you Were Born to Write: Everything You Need to (Finally) Get Your Wisdom into the Page and into the World.*[85]

And finally, my daughters—Sophia, Michaela and Giordana—the next generation of professional working mothers and my purpose in life. I love you more than infinity.

About the Author

Elizabeth Kagan Arleo MD, FACR, FSBI, FAAWR

Dr. Elizabeth Kagan Arleo is a Professor of Radiology at Weill Cornell Medical College and an Attending Radiologist at the New York-Presbyterian Hospital. In 2019, she served as the President of

the American Association for Women in Radiology (AAWR). She is also the Editor-in-Chief of the journal *Clinical Imaging*.

Dr. Arleo has received multiple honors and awards, including the 2017 Laurie H. Glimcher M.D. Award for Excellence in Mentoring Women Faculty from Weill Cornell, the 2018 Distinguished Educator Award from the NY Roentgen Society, and the 2022 Alice Ettinger Distinguished Achievement Award recognizing lifetime achievements and lasting contributions to radiology from the AAWR.

Dr. Arleo considers her greatest professional legacy to be her compassionate care of patients and her advocacy for improved family/medical leave in radiology. Personally, she is also a mother of three, and a writer and runner. *First, Eat Your Frog: And Other Pearls for Professional Working Mothers* is her first book.

Endnotes

1 Richard Chang, "Moms feel overwhelmed by responsibilities: poll," Reuters, June 15, 2011; J Gross, "American's Mothers Are in Crisis," *The New York Times*, February 4, 2021; Laura Vanderkam, *168 Hours: You Have More Time Than You Think. Portfolio Publishers.*, May 31, 2011.

2 Jessica Grose, "American's Mothers Are in Crisis," *The New York Times*. February 4, 2021; www.nytimes.com/2021/02/04/parenting/working-moms-mental-health-coronavirus.html.

3 Carol Dweck, *Mindset: The New Psychology of Success* (Ballantine, 2007).

4 J Henley, "Why we shouldn't eat frogs' legs," *The Guardian*, August 6, 2009.

5 Arnold Lobel, *Frog and Toad Together*, (HarperCollins, 1979).

6 L Ruppanner, "Understanding the mental load, what it is and how to get it under control," ABC News. September 13, 2017.

7 "Reduce stress – 'Eat the frog!' The National Counselling Society; nationalcounsellingsociety.org

8 "Exploring the Second Shift," Inter-university Consortium for Political and Social Research (ICPSR); icpsr.umich.edu

9 M Causse, et al., "Facing successfully high mental workload and stressors: An fMRI study," Human Brain Mapping, February 15, 2022;43(3):1011-1031. doi: 10.1002/hbm.25703. Epub 2021 Nov 5. PMID: 34738280; PMCID: PMC8764488.

10 Gretchen Rubin, *The Four Tendencies: The Indispensable Personality Profiles That Reveal How to Make Your Life Better (and Other People's Lives Better, Too)* (Hodder & Stoughton, 2018), page 8

11 "What is decision fatigue?" *Medical News Today*, July 6, 2020.

12 Laura Vanderkam, "Weekly relationship priorities," February 7, 2017; lauravanderkam.com

13 "Time is the most valuable thing a man can spend," Coaching Positive Performance; coachingpositiveperformance.com

14 Greg McKeon, *Essentialism: The Disciplined Pursuit of Less* (Crown, 2020).

15 Ibid.

16 J Howarth, "Time Spent Using Smartphones (2022 Statistics)," *Exploding Topics*, September 16, 2022.

17 R Zalani, "Screen Time Statistics: Your Smartphone Is Hurting You," *Elite Content Marketer*, October 8, 2022.

18 Tiny Buddha: Simple wisdom for complex lives; tinybuddha.com.

19 J Willink, *Discipline Equals Freedom: Field Manual* (St. Martin's Press,2017).

20 JE Engel, "The First Commandment of Strategic Planning: Don't Fail to Plan," *Forbes*, May 29, 2020.

21 McKeon, *Ibid.*

22 *Ibid.*

23 P Schwartz, "Your Future in 5 East Steps: Wired Guide to Personal Scenario Planning Step 1," *Wired.* July 20, 2009.

24 Oscar Wilde: "To expect the unexpected shows a thoroughly modern intellect," *An Ideal Husband* (1895), Act III.

25 "Defense.gov News Transcript: DoD News Briefing – Secretary Rumsfeld and Gen. Myers, United States Department of Defense (defense.gov)," February 12, 2002.

26 "What is GTD?" gettingthingsdone.com.

27 "The Tools and Resources You Need to Win at Work and Success at Life," Full Focus.com.

28 S Berg, "COVID-19 puts new emphasis on need for physician burnout solutions," American Medical Association, November 16, 2021.

29 A Vitali, "Study finds 'burnout epidemic' for working women two years into pandemic," NBC News. April 26, 2022.

30 M Hyatt, D Harkavy. *Living Forward: A Proven Plan to Stop Drifting and Get the Life You Want* (Baker Books 2016).

31 G McKeon, Essentialism Academy, "21-Day Essentialism Challenge."

32 R Lane, "A New Way to Set New Year's Resolutions," *iGrad, Behavioral Finance*, December 2020.

33 Laura Vanderkam, *Juliet's School of Possibilities* (Portfolio Publishers, 2019), page 83.

34 M Dorsey, "Be Fearless…or at Least Appear to Be," RadEqual, June 26, 2018.

35 *Ibid.*

36 Oxford Learner's Dictionaries, Meeting.

37 A Molinsky, "When It's Worth Having a Meeting Before Your Meeting," *Harvard Business Review*, October 28, 2016.

38 Impostor Syndrome. Definitions from Oxford Languages.

39 Elizabeth K Arleo, et al., "Tackling impostor syndrome: A multidisciplinary approach," *Clinical Imaging*, June 2021;74:170-172. doi: 10.1016/j. clinimag.2020.12.035. Epub 2021 Jan 14. PMID: 33478806.

40 L Geall, "12 successful women on impostor syndrome and self-doubt," *Stylist.*

41 *Ibid.*

42 "Sheryl Sandberg's Secret to Success & Breaking The Glass Ceiling," *The Economic Times.* August 28, 2021.

43 John Maxwell, *Leadership Gold: Lessons I've Learned from a Lifetime of Leading* (Thomas Nelson Publishers, 2008).

44 Elizabeth K Arleo, et al., *Ibid.*

45 JA Allen, N Lehmann-Willenbrock, N Landowski, "Linking Pre-meeting Communication to Meeting Effectiveness," *Psychology Faculty Publications*, Department of Psychology, University of Nebraska at Omaha, 2014.

46 Arleo J. Personal communication. 2022.

47 General George Patton: "A good plan today is better than a perfect one tomorrow," Quotes from the past; quotesfromthepast.com/a-good-plan-today-is-better-than-a-perfect-plan-tomorrow/

48 Aileron, "Why Good Is Better Than Perfect," Forbes, August 19, 2014.

49 *Ibid.*

50 E Lawrence, "The Psychology Behind The Fear of Missing Out (FOMO)," *Forbes Health*, September 30, 2022.

51 "Don't Let 'Perfect' Be the Enemy of 'Good,'" *Harvard Business Review*, February 14, 2020.

52 *Ibid.*

53 H Demsetz, "Information and efficiency: another viewpoint," The Journal of Law And Economics, 1969, 12(1), 1-22.

54 Laura Vanderkam, *Juliet's School of Possibilities* (Portfolio Publishers, 2019), page 83.

55 CE Bender, et al., 2019 ACR Commission on Human Resources Workforce Survey, *Journal of the American College of Radiology*, 2020 May;17(5):673-675. doi: 10.1016/j.jacr.2020.01.012. Epub 2020 Feb 14. PMID: 32068008.

56 K Magudia, et al., "Pathway and Gateway Issues Affecting Gender Diversity in Academic Radiology Department Chairs," Submitted September 2022 for *Journal of the American College of Radiology* for consideration for publication, decision pending.

57 R Jacobson, "Why Girls Apologize Too Much," *Child Mind Institute*, September 7, 2021.

58 *Ibid.*

59 Charles Duhigg, *The Power of Habit: What we do in life and business* (Random House Trade Paperbacks, 2014).

60 Wang Yip, "Are You an Adder or a Subtracter? October 19, 2020; https://wangyip.medium.com/are-you-an-adder-or-a-subtracter-1a5acbf25182.

61 C Castrillon, "How Women Can Stop Apologizing And Take Their Power Back," *Forbes*, July 14, 2019.

62 CM Rumack, "Women Don't Ask, *Journal of American College of Radiology*, 2016 Jan;13(1):90-2. doi: 10.1016/j.jacr.2015.08.010. Epub 2015 Oct 27. PMID: 26514107.

63 *Ibid.*

64 *Ibid.*

65 LP Frankel, *Nice Girls Don't Get the Corner Office* (Business Plus, 2010)

66 K Parker, JM Horowitz, R. Stepler, "Americans see different expectations for men and women," Pew Research Center, December 5, 2017

67 M Manning, "Let It Go – Exploring And Escaping The 'Good Girl' Syndrome," *Huffington Post*, February 22, 2014

68 Sheryl Sandberg, *Lean In: Women, Work, and the Will to Lead* (Knopf, 2013), Introduction.

69 K Magudia, et al., "Childbearing and Family Leave Policies for Resident Physicians at Top Training Institutions," *Journal of the American Medical Association*, 2018 Dec 11;320(22):2372-2374. doi: 10.1001/jama.2018.14414. PMID: 30535210; PMCID: PMC6583066.

70 Elizabeth K Arleo, et al., "Family and Medical Leave Act Should Be Applicable to All Radiologists and Radiation Oncologists," *Journal of American College of Radiology*, 2015 Oct;12(10):1125-6. doi: 10.1016/j.jacr.2015.04.013. Epub 2015 Jun 27. PMID: 26130222.

71 Elizabeth K Arleo, et al., "Utilization of the Family and Medical Leave Act in Radiology Practices According to the 2016 ACR Commission on Human Resources Workforce Survey, *Journal of American College of Radiology*, 2016 Dec;13(12 Pt A):1440-1446. doi: 10.1016/j.jacr.2016.08.023. PMID: 27916110.

72 Elizabeth K Arleo, "Female Editors-in-Chief of Radiology Journals Do Exist," *Journal of American College of Radiology*, 2019 Jun;16(6):780. doi: 10.1016/j.jacr.2019.03.003. PMID: 31171139.

73 Brendan Murphy, "AMA backs stronger leave policies for medical students, doctors," American Medical Association (AMA), November 16, 2022, https:// www.ama-assn.org/medical-students/medical-student-health/ama-backs-stronger-leave-policies-medical-students-doctors.

74 JA Schmidt, L Shumow, HZ Kackar-Cam, "Does Mindset Intervention Predict Students' Daily Experience in Classrooms? A Comparison of Seventh and Ninth Graders'Trajectories," *Journal of Youth and Adolescence*, 2017 Mar;46(3):582-602. doi: 10.1007/s10964-016-0489-z. Epub 2016 Apr 22. PMID: 27106713.

75 Gretchen Rubin, "Refinement of My Earth-Shattering Happiness Formula," February 12, 2007; https://gretchenrubin.com/articles/a-refinement-of-my-earth-shattering-happiness-formula/

76 S Briggs, "25 Ways to Develop a Growth Mindset," Open Colleges, February 10, 2015.

77 *Ibid.*

78 Laura Vanderkam, *Juliet's School of Possibilities* (Portfolio Publishers, 2019), page 83.

79 Castrillon, *Ibid.*

80 "Rumack, *Ibid.*

81 Carol Dweck, "Carol Dweck Revisits the 'Growth Mindset," *Education Week*, September 22, 2015

82 David Allen, *Getting Things Done: The Art of Stress-Free Productivity* (Piatkus Books, 2015)

83 Nancy Bardacke, *Mindful Birthing: Training the Mind, Body, and Heart for Childbirth and Beyond* (HarperOne Publishers, 2012)

84 Tiffany Dufu, *Drop the Ball: Achieving More by Doing Less.* (Flatiron Books, 2017).

85 Kelly Notaras, *The Book You Were Born to Write: Everything You Need to (Finally) Get Your Wisdom onto the Page and into the World* (Carlsbad: Hay House Inc, 2018).